CHANGE IS P(
THE SEVEN ST..... ..
HEALING TRAUMA

BY MICHAEL MAISEY

SW
Publishers

Published by
SW Publishers Ltd
9 High Street
Wellington, England
TA21 8QT
swpublishers.co.uk

ISBN: 978-1-39998996-1

Printed in England

DEDICATION

This book is dedicated to the boy I once was, who carried
so much pain, and to every person who has suffered.
I wrote this with the hope of reducing human suffering,
offering comfort and a path to healing. May it
inspire us all to find peace and the courage to
believe in a better future.

DISCLAIMER

This book is based on my personal recovery from trauma, which in many ways followed a very different path to traditional methods of healing. The insights I share are drawn from my lived experience and are not intended to replace professional medical, psychological, or therapeutic advice. I am not a doctor or mental health professional.

If you're struggling with trauma or mental health challenges, I encourage you to seek support from qualified professionals or trusted organizations that can provide appropriate care. Always consult a professional for advice specific to your situation.

TABLE OF CONTENTS

INTRODUCTION

It was a cold November morning in 2020, just days after my daughter Savanna was born. I stood by the window, holding her tiny, bundled-up body in my arms, feeling her warmth against my chest. The world outside was crisp and still, and as I looked out, I felt a wave of gratitude so powerful it nearly took my breath away.

I'd done it. The life I once thought impossible was now my reality. I had the home I'd always dreamed of, a beautiful family, over a decade of sobriety, and a sense of peace I never believed I'd find. Life was better than anything I could have imagined during those dark days when survival felt like my only option.

And yet, as I stood there, it all felt surreal. Somehow, after a childhood filled with trauma, years spent battling addiction, prison sentences, and even a failed suicide attempt, I was here. Holding my daughter in my arms, living a life that, for most of my early years, felt like a far-off dream.

If I'm honest, the odds of me making it out were slim. Growing up on a council estate where opportunity was scarce and survival was the priority, most of the people I knew were consumed by the same cycles of addiction, violence, and despair. I suspect I'm the only one from my estate—or perhaps even my entire area—who truly managed to break free. It doesn't make sense, really. How did I make it here? I ask myself that question often.

But as I looked beyond my world—beyond the green fields and the warmth of my home—I couldn't ignore what I saw. The same broken systems that had shaped my childhood were still thriving, still causing untold pain. Since 2007, when I first began this journey, I've dedicated myself to understanding and addressing the root causes of suffering. From the work I've done in prisons, the countless people I've met through my charity, The CIP Project, and the stories I've heard whilst delivering my work across the UK, Ireland, and Europe, the same grim picture has come into sharp focus. These systems aren't just failing—they're perpetuating harm. And that's a truth I can't turn away from.

Addiction is at an all-time high. Suicide rates are climbing. Crime continues to spread, and prison rehabilitation is still a revolving door. Mental health struggles are at epidemic levels, and children from low-income households, often eligible for free school meals, are being excluded from mainstream education at alarming rates. And let's not forget our military veterans—the men and women who have served their country only to return and find themselves abandoned, many homeless on the streets of cities across the UK.

These issues are not isolated—they are interconnected. They tell the story of systems that don't just fail but actively harm the very people they're supposed to protect. It's a grim reality, but it's one we must face if we're ever going to create meaningful change.

The suffering I've seen—both in my own life and in the lives of others—keeps repeating, generation after generation. At the heart of so many of these issues is trauma— emotional, mental, physical, or sexual. If we don't address this pain, the cycle will never end. Real change starts with facing it.

It felt deeply unfair to stand in this place of peace, knowing how much pain still exists in the world. I couldn't shake the question: *What kind of man would I be if I didn't do something about it?*

This book is my answer.

It's not just a reflection on my own journey from trauma to transformation—it's my offering to the world. A parting gift, if you like, filled with everything I've learned about healing, growth, and change.

When I wrote *Young Offender*, it was about sharing my story up until 2014, closing that chapter of my life. But as I reflected, I realized there were so many valuable lessons left untold—lessons that could help others. This book is my final word on the subject.

I don't expect miracles, nor do I assume these words will change the world overnight. But I believe in planting seeds. Some seeds take years, even decades, to grow. They may not sprout until long after I'm gone, but my hope is that by sharing my story, someone, somewhere, might find the courage to change their own life. And perhaps, one day, the ripple effects of those changes will reach the systems that so desperately need reform.

I hold a vision for a better future—a future where prisons are not places of punishment but environments of safety and growth, providing the tools people need to truly change their lives. A future where schools offer spaces of support and security, nurturing children not only academically but emotionally, helping them navigate their challenges with care. A world where access to tools for personal self-development is not a privilege reserved for the wealthy, but a basic right for everyone, regardless of their financial circumstances. And a society that can recognize, understand, and support those of us recovering from trauma, ensuring that healing isn't something we stumble upon, but something we're guided toward.

This book is for the people still suffering, for those caught in cycles of pain and despair. It's for the children growing up in broken systems and for the adults still carrying wounds from their past. Most of all, it's for anyone who dares to believe that change is possible—not just for themselves, but for the world.

If this book plants even one seed of hope, it will have been worth it.

CHAPTER 1

SAFETY

"A journey of healing cannot begin until we feel safe enough to take off our masks and let down the walls we've built around our hearts."

Everything we think we know about healing from trauma is wrong. Around the world, the systems we've put in place to address trauma—whether it's through addiction treatment, mental health care, prison rehabilitation, or crisis intervention—are failing. Why? Because we're only treating the symptoms, not the root causes. We're too focused on the behaviors: the addiction, the self-harm, the incidents, the crimes, or the suicide attempts. We rush to treat these visible wounds without first establishing the one thing that makes true healing possible: safety.

No one can heal while they're stuck in survival mode.

The scars, memories, and pain that trauma leaves behind are overwhelming, and without a sense of safety, the very thought of facing them is terrifying. For those of us who've lived with trauma, true healing isn't just about therapy sessions or coping techniques. It's about building a safe foundation—one that allows us to lower our defenses, release the constant fear, and finally start the real work of healing.

Yet this fundamental need for safety is often over-looked. And that's why, despite billions spent on programs and interventions, we continue to see rising rates of addiction, mental health struggles, suicides, and reoffending. Our collective failure to prioritize safety is keeping millions trapped in cycles of pain and despair.

For me, finding safety was the first and most essential step in my own journey. But before I could get there, I lived through years of chaos that taught me how it feels to be truly unsafe. Those experiences hardened me, made me believe that any sense of safety was an illusion.

Consider, for example, a child labeled as "naughty" at school. Statistics show that most children excluded from school face issues at home. Yet, our typical response is to send them back to the very environment that's causing their distress, making the problem worse. These kids often grow into troubled teens who then end up in prisons where they're locked up for 23 hours a day with no real rehabilitation. We're offering them less safety, not more.

And it's not just schools and prisons. Look at military veterans with PTSD. On the front line, they have structure, routine, and a sense of safety among their brothers. When they come home, all of that is stripped away, often leading them to turn to alcohol and drugs.

The same goes for rehab centers, children's homes, special education schools, and even traditional therapy settings. Without safety, the very foundation of healing is missing, leaving people stuck in survival mode, unable to move forward.

This issue isn't isolated to schools, prisons, and our military—it's everywhere. By shining a light on this, we can begin to fix the problem. No matter the setting, the principle remains the same: healing can only begin when safety is established. Yet, globally, we continue to overlook this essential truth.

Until we find a space secure enough to let our guard down, healing will remain out of reach. And this is the truth we need to address—on an individual level, in our communities, and as a global society.

If we can't create safety, we can't create change. But when we start with safety, we open the door to transformation. I'll share more about my own story and the lessons I've learned, showing just how powerful and life-changing finding safety can be.

THE EARLY LESSONS OF INSTABILITY

As far back as I can remember, my life was shaped by chaos and instability. By the time I was just a year old, I had already lived in five different homes. We started in a flat on School Road in Hounslow, then moved to a women's refuge on Church Street in Old Isleworth. From there, it was a council flat on the Green Dragon Estate in Brentford, followed by another women's shelter near Kew Gardens. Eventually, we found ourselves on the Ivybridge Estate in Isleworth, a place that, for a short while, offered a small glimmer of safety.

But the instability didn't begin with me—it started long before, when I was still in my mother's womb. My father was violent toward her even then. His anger loomed over her every moment, and she carried me under that shadow of fear. I can only imagine the weight of it, trying to protect a child who hadn't even been born yet.

When I was just weeks old, my mother made a decision that still takes my breath away. She wanted me christened in the Catholic Church, but she knew my father would never allow it. So, she fled, traveling all the way to a church in Luton, where she could perform this simple act of faith and hope in secret.

It wasn't just the location that made the day unusual. The local priest was away on a pilgrimage, so my christening was performed by the archbishop himself—a moment that should have been marked by joy and celebration. But there were no family gatherings, no proud relatives or godparents surrounding the altar. Just my mum and one witness—a young woman who had grown up with her in Nazareth Lodge Children's Home in Ireland. Two women, bound by shared pain and resilience, standing together in a quiet church as the archbishop poured water over my head and whispered blessings for my future.

Looking back now, I feel the ache of that moment. My mum wasn't just christening me that day; she was trying to carve out a piece of stability in a world that had offered her none. She was fighting to give me a chance at something better, even if the odds were stacked against her.

When we finally settled on the Ivybridge Estate, it felt like a brief pause in a life defined by struggle. My father, violent and unpredictable, couldn't find us there. For a while, we were safe. But safety, as I would come to learn, was always fleeting.

Even so, I look back on those early years with a deep admiration for my mother. As a child, I couldn't understand the full weight of what she carried or the courage it took to keep moving forward. But now, I see her strength. In the face of relentless hardship, she never gave up trying to protect me. She fought, not just for herself, but for her son.

My mother's story was marked by instability and hardship long before I was born. She was an Irish immigrant, born into an Irish Traveller family at the side of a road in Dublin. Our family name was Maughan, and we originally came from County Mayo, traveling all around Ireland. The Travellers were a people of resilience, carrying their culture and traditions through a history of oppression. But safety was always fleeting.

When visiting the North, which was under British occupation, the British social services came to the camp. They saw children who were dirty, barefoot, and malnourished. Without understanding or compassion for the lives these families lived, they decided that all the children should be taken into the care system. My grandmother, Winnie, fought hard to stop it from happening, but the Travelling people of Ireland had very few rights. They were a marginalized group, oppressed by systems that saw them as a problem to be solved, rather than a people to be respected.

At one point in Irish history, it was illegal to identify as an Irish Traveller. Imagine that—a whole race of people made invisible by law, denied the right to their identity. My family carried this weight. The lack of safety they experienced, combined with nearly 700 years of Ireland being under British occupation, was the backdrop to my mother's childhood.

When she was just a girl, she was taken into the care system. For her, this meant being sent to Nazareth Lodge in Belfast, a place that has since become infamous for its systemic abuse of children. The details of what happened behind those walls are too grim to comprehend fully, but the scars it left on the children who passed through are undeniable.

At just sixteen years old, my mother fled Ireland and came to London. What was she searching for? Safety.

What did she find? Prejudice and hostility.

The signs on hotels and bars said it all: *No Blacks. No Dogs. No Irish.* Imagine arriving in a country seeking refuge, only to be greeted with rejection and exclusion. Was her subconscious desire for healing playing out as she tried to escape the trauma of her own upbringing? Perhaps. Instead of finding safety, she encountered a society that, at the time, was unwilling to provide it.

This deep need for safety—the longing for it and the constant lack of it—seeped into her life and, in turn, into mine. Her struggle to find security shaped everything about the way I grew up. The systems that had oppressed her, the traumas she carried from her own childhood, and the prejudice she faced as an Irish Traveller and an immigrant—they all landed on her shoulders.

Yet, despite it all, she kept going. My mother's strength, her will to survive and protect me, is something I carry with me to this day. But I also carry the weight of her story, the lack of safety that defined her life and mine. These are the stories we must tell, because only in bringing them to light can we begin to break the cycles that have held us captive for generations.

By the time I was a teenager, my own life mirrored the instability my mother had endured. It was as though I was living out the same painful script, following the same broken paths she had walked. Just as my mother was uprooted from her Traveller family and shuffled through systems that failed to protect her, I found myself caught in those same revolving doors.

From children's homes to bail hostels, young offenders institutions to foster families, each new place carried the promise of safety and stability but delivered something far different. The children's homes, meant to provide refuge, were breeding grounds for bullying, sexual predators, and peer pressure. I saw kids, some younger than me, pulled into a cycle of drug use and petty crime, not because they were bad, but because that's what these places bred—desperation and survival.

The young offenders institutions were no better. They weren't places for rehabilitation; they were training grounds for future criminals. Locked up for 23 hours a day, we had nothing to do but sit in our cells and share every detail of our crimes: what we did, how we got caught, and what we'd do differently next time. It was like a college or university campus, except the only lessons were in crime, and the professors were the inmates themselves.

And then there were the foster families. They took us in for three to six months at a time—a temporary measure, never a permanent solution. Each new placement uprooted me again and again, adding another layer of instability to an already chaotic life. It wasn't that the foster parents didn't care, but the system itself wasn't built to provide lasting safety. It was a revolving door that created fleeting connections, not real homes.

Are we noticing the pattern? The same systems that failed my mum—stripping her of safety, stability, and connection—were now failing me. Her childhood was shaped by instability, a relentless search for safety that was always just out of reach. And now here I was, living the same story.

The children's homes. The hostels. The institutions. The foster families. Each one a failed system, offering promises it could never deliver. And through it all, the instability seeped deeper into me, shaping how I saw the world and my place in it.

The weight of these broken systems wasn't just something I carried—it shaped who I was becoming. And until we acknowledge how these cycles continue to repeat, generation after generation, the suffering will never stop.

When we're supporting those who've experienced trauma, especially young people in schools, the justice or care systems, it's crucial to understand that consistency in care is key to their recovery. As a youth justice worker, social worker, child psychologist, or teacher, the role you play is more than just professional; for those you help, you become a beacon of trust. But here's the challenge—these roles are often temporary. Just as a bond begins to form, and a young per- son starts to feel safe enough to open up, the person might move on due to the limits of the job's duration. This can feel like a repeating cycle of trust built and trust broken, which isn't conducive to healing.

On top of this, many of these workers are stretched thin, overworked and underpaid. While it's not the fault of these dedicated individuals, this situation can unintentionally signal to those healing from trauma that their struggles might not be a priority, undermining their sense of safety even further. Statistics show that high caseloads and turnover in these professions can lead to less effective support for trauma survivors, who require consistent and focused care to navigate their healing journey effectively.

How much instability and lack of safety does it take before we realize that what we're doing isn't working?

This isn't just my story; it's a pattern playing out globally. Trauma survivors are shuffled between systems that promise help but fail to address the root of the issue.

Instability is more than just a lack of a permanent address. It's a wound that shapes how we see the world and how we see ourselves. When safety is missing, the damage doesn't just stop—it repeats, again and again. For me, that repetition was clear: the more unstable my environment, the more deeply I normalized chaos.

Perhaps you can relate. Have you ever experienced inconsistency from people meant to care and support you?

Have you ever felt like things were unstable and insecure? How did it make you feel? Was this a place where you could feel safe enough to heal?

The hard truth is, that healing doesn't happen in survival mode.

Trauma wires our brains to see the world as unsafe and unpredictable. For many, this starts in childhood, leaving scars that can last a lifetime. Studies show that adverse childhood experiences (ACEs)—like emotional, physical, or sexual abuse, neglect, or growing up with parents who are alcoholics, absent, or abusive—are strongly linked to lifelong struggles with physical, mental, and emotional health. Even the more subtle forms of abuse, like the emotional pain of withdrawn love or the relentless drip of constant criticism, can leave wounds just as deep as physical or sexual abuse.

What makes it worse is how relentless some of this can be. With physical or sexual abuse, it might—though not always—come in sporadic moments, giving the child brief chances to recover. But emotional and mental abuse? That's often a daily battle, stretching over years, leaving scars that are harder to see but no less real. These experiences create a world that feels inherently unsafe, shaping how we interact with others and how we see ourselves.

When we live in that kind of unsafe world, it's easy to question the validity of our pain, especially when we start comparing it to others. But I always say, there's no league table in trauma. Your experience is your experience—valid, true, and deeply personal. When we minimize what we've been through by thinking, "Well, it wasn't as bad as what someone else endured," we unintentionally build an invisible barrier between ourselves and the first step of healing. By dismissing the significance of our own pain, we shut down the possibility of moving forward. Whether it's a momentary wound or years of subtle, grinding harm, every experience matters. Recognizing that truth—and finding safety to express it—is the only way to begin dismantling the patterns that trauma leaves behind.

We see the consequences of unaddressed trauma ripple through every corner of life—in prisons, veteran support programs, addiction recovery centers, and schools. The pattern is the same across these environments. People aren't just struggling with behaviors or symptoms; they're wrestling with the pain of a world that never felt safe. This is even reflected in the statistics. A report from the UK Ministry of Justice indicates that prisoners who complete mandatory rehabilitation programs reoffend at nearly the same rate as those who don't. Similarly, children from broken homes face higher rates of exclusion from schools, underscoring the same issue: these programs and systems often focus on correcting behavior without first creating a sense of safety. Without establishing safety, it's impossible to begin addressing the deeper wounds that drive the behavior in the first place.

I know I keep repeating this point, but it truly needs to be drilled home to understand the full implications. This is true not just for veterans with PTSD or people battling addiction, but also for troubled school kids from broken homes. In my own experience, from the age of 5 until I left prison at 18, not a single social worker, teacher, youth justice worker, probation officer, prison officer, or police officer ever asked me if I felt safe. No one took the time to establish any sense of safety with me. Instead, they jumped straight into trying to resolve the problems, approaching each situation with complete emotional detachment from everything that had happened before the incident. They focused only on the surface symptoms—substance abuse, anger, depression—without addressing the underlying pain. Without establishing safety first, healing can't truly begin. It's like trying to grow a plant in toxic soil—it just doesn't work.

What we need, what every person in pain needs, is to feel safe first. Safety allows walls to come down and opens the door to honesty and healing. Whether it's in a prison cell, a rehab centre, or a support group, creating that sense of safety is the first step. Without it, we're just managing problems, not solving them, leaving people stuck in cycles of survival instead of opening the door to transformation.

MASLOW'S HIERARCHY AND THE NEED FOR SAFETY

The need for safety isn't a new discovery—we've known about it for decades. Abraham Maslow laid it out clearly in the 1940s with his "Hierarchy of Needs," a foundational concept in psychology. At its base are our most essential needs: food, water, shelter. Just above that is safety—the point where we can finally stop looking over our shoulders and feel secure enough to grow. Without this foundation, nothing else—healing, growth, or recovery—can take hold.

What's striking is that learning about Maslow's theory is a fundamental part of becoming a therapist or psychologist. It's one of the first things most professionals in these fields are taught. They understand that without addressing basic needs, no real progress can be made. Yet despite this foundational knowledge, we still haven't implemented it properly into our systems.

Take war veterans, for example. Many start treatment for PTSD while they're still in the military, surrounded by an environment where seeking help is often stigmatized, viewed as weakness. They're expected to confront their trauma while still immersed in a culture that demands strength at all costs. How can they begin to heal when they're stuck in the very environment that caused their pain?

It's the same in the prison system, where rehabilitation programs operate in environments that strip people of their safety and dignity. Prisoners are expected to change their behavior while living in fear, constantly on edge. It's the same in poor communities, where survival is a daily fight and asking for help is seen as a luxury or, worse, a failure.

Similarly, children from broken homes who are excluded from school often find themselves expected to heal within the home where they experienced trauma, or worse, in a community surrounded by other troubled children. This places them in a cycle of stress and adversity, making true healing a significant challenge. Can you see the pattern yet? Can you see the bigger problem I'm trying to show you?

I wish I could lend you my eyes so you could see exactly what I see. We're asking people to heal in environments that keep them in survival mode. We're asking people to recover while surrounded by the very forces that perpetuate their trauma. It's like telling someone to mend their wounds while they're still on the battlefield.

This isn't just about individuals—it's a systemic failure. Without safety, veterans can't heal. Prisoners can't rehabilitate. People in poor communities can't break free. Homeless individuals can't rebuild their lives.

We know this. Therapists and psychologists know this. Maslow showed us decades ago. And yet, here we are, still asking people to grow roots in toxic soil, to climb out of survival mode without giving them the foundation they need.

The truth is, nothing meaningful can happen until safety is established. Without it, every effort is like building on quicksand. Healing starts at the base of the pyramid—with stability, with security, with safety. Until we truly integrate this understanding into our systems, the cycles will keep repeating, and people will remain trapped in the very structures meant to help them.

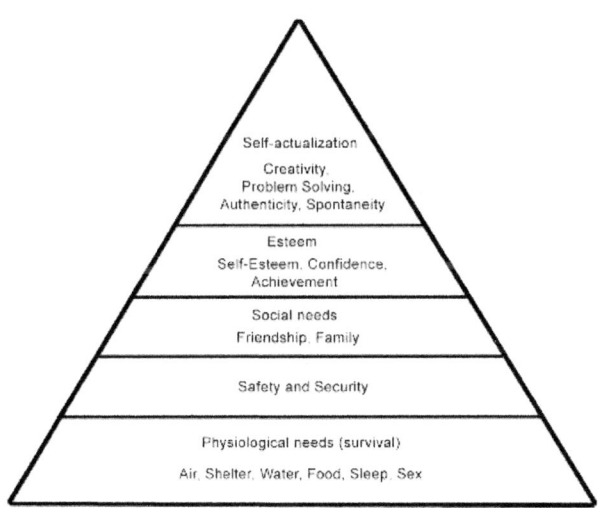

THERE IS HOPE

In 2007, I walked into my first AA meeting in a small
church on the Antrim Road in North Belfast. I was 25
years old—an English guy with a skinhead, an attitude
problem, and a deep belief that I didn't belong anywhere.
I was carrying so much pain, but I hid it behind a tough
exterior.

The people in that room were nothing like me. They
had thick Irish accents, they looked older, wiser, and their
lives seemed a world away from mine. I had every reason to
feel out of place. And yet, I didn't.

For the first time in as long as I could remember, I felt
safe. It wasn't the kind of safety that comes from locks or
alarms—it was the kind that comes from being seen, from
being understood. There was no judgment in that room, no

one looking down on me. There were no lectures or empty words of encouragement. Instead, there were stories—raw, unpolished, and painfully honest stories from people who had been where I was.

They weren't trying to fix me or tell me what to do. They didn't need to. Their stories were enough. When they spoke about their pain, I recognized mine. When they spoke about their shame, I saw my own reflected back. And for the first time in my life, I started to believe that maybe I wasn't broken beyond repair.

Something shifted in me that night. It wasn't a miracle or an instant transformation, but it was real. That shared experience, that sense of being truly understood, cracked something open in me. I let my guard down just a little. Enough to keep going back.

Those meetings became my lifeline. That feeling of safety, of being in a space where no one judged and everyone understood, wasn't just comforting—it was life-changing. It gave me the courage to take a step forward, then another, and another.

That lesson—about the power of being seen, of shared experience—has stayed with me ever since. It's what led me to create *The CIP Project*, a place where people can come exactly as they are, without fear of judgment. A place where safety isn't just a concept; it's the foundation of everything we do.

Because I know what it's like to feel lost, to believe you don't belong anywhere. And I know how powerful it is to find even a flicker of hope in the darkness. If there's one thing I've learned, it's this: no matter how far gone you feel, there's always a way back. And it starts with feeling safe enough to take that first step.

In 2021, my prison outreach team and I delivered a workshop inside HMP Exeter. The room was filled with men who had spent years in survival mode—hardened by life, by the system, by everything that had gone wrong. They came in guarded, sceptical, their walls so firmly up you could feel it in the air. The tension was thick, like a silent challenge: *What can you possibly tell me that I haven't already heard?*

But here's the thing about my prison outreach team— we're not professionals in suits with clipboards and theories. Every single person on my team has served time. Every single one of them knows what it feels like to be sitting in those chairs, wondering if life will ever get better. Lived experience isn't just part of the job—it's the foundation of it. It's non-negotiable because we know it's the key to creating the kind of safety these men need.

When my team introduced themselves, you could feel the energy in the room shift. They didn't speak from a script; they spoke from the heart. They didn't offer solutions or pretend to have all the answers. They shared their stories—honest, raw, and full of the kind of pain that only someone who's been there can truly understand.

And the men listened. Really listened.

It didn't take long before the stories started flowing. Men who hadn't spoken about their pain in years—maybe decades—began to open up. They talked about regrets they'd buried, guilt they couldn't shake, and dreams they were too scared to admit they still had.

The walls came down. You could feel it—something real, something powerful. A sense of safety, of trust, of possibility. For a moment, these men weren't prisoners or statistics. They were human beings, seen and heard for perhaps the first time in a very long time.

After the session, a group of prison officers came up to me. Their amazement was written all over their faces.

"We've been trying to get through to them for months, even years," one officer said. "They've never opened up like this before. How did you do it?"

The answer is simple: lived experience.

It's not about lectures or programs designed in offices far removed from the realities of prison life. It's about creating a space where people can see themselves in you, where they know they're not being judged or looked down on. It's about showing them that change is possible because you've lived it.

That day in Exeter wasn't just another workshop. It was a reminder of the power of connection, the strength of vulnerability, and the way lived experience can break through even the toughest walls. It's not magic, but it can feel like it. And it's the reason I do this work—because I've seen what happens when someone finally believes they're not alone and that change is possible.

I've seen this happen so many times—at our events in Devon, in prisons, in corporate workshops. People show up with fear and scepticism written all over their faces. They sit quietly, arms crossed, questioning why they even bothered coming. You can almost hear their inner voices: *This won't help me. What's the point?*

But then something happens.

They're met with something they didn't expect: real-life stories. Not from therapists or professionals who've read about trauma in books, but from people who've lived it. People who've been broken, who've clawed their way out of the darkness, and who now stand there, sharing their truth.

And slowly, the fear melts away. The walls come down. Trust begins to grow.

I've seen it in rooms full of men hardened by life, unsure if change is even possible. I've seen it in corporate offices, where executives and employees alike come in guarded, masks firmly in place. But when those stories are shared—when the masks drop—it's like a switch is flipped. A sense of safety is created, and in that safety, change becomes possible.

Because safety isn't just about physical security. It's about knowing you're not alone. It's about hearing someone say, *"I've been where you are, and I've made it through."* That kind of safety is life-changing.

In 2019, after my book *Young Offender* was released, I was invited to the Houses of Parliament to share my story. I found myself in a place of power, speaking on behalf of the powerless. I was speaking about what needs to change in our prison system and in social care. After my talk, I was taken into a private meeting room with key decision-makers in government.

One of them looked at me and said, "Michael, it's amazing how you've turned your life around. We'd really like to hear your thoughts on how we could change things."

I paused for a moment, then said, "I could answer your question, but maybe I could ask you something instead?" They nodded, encouraging me to continue.

So, I asked, "How many of you in this room have been to prison? Grown up on a council estate? Attended a state school?"

Not a single hand went up.

"So," I said, "most of you were privately educated, perhaps even went to boarding schools. And here you are, trying to fix a problem you've never experienced."

The room went quiet. Heads lowered. I could see the weight of my words settling in.

"What I'm proposing," I said, "is that you bring people with lived experience into the conversation before decisions are made. People who understand these systems from the inside. People who have felt their failures firsthand."

After a long silence, one of them spoke. "It's so simple," they said. "But so true."

I walked out of that room hoping my words had landed somewhere, hoping that a seed had been planted.

Some years later, I heard that the Home Office had set up a lived experience team to advise on these issues.

I'm not claiming credit for that—it was likely the result of many voices, not just mine. But I share this story to give you hope.

Because when we centre lived experience, when we create safety through shared stories, we create the conditions for real change. It's not just comforting—it's transformative. It's the foundation upon which hope is built, and it's how we begin to heal what's broken.

Change is coming. I know it because I've seen it. And I believe in it, because I've lived it.

FINDING SAFETY IN KINDNESS

When I was released from prison at eighteen years old, the first job I managed to get was as a street sweeper. It wasn't glamorous, and I knew full well it would come with judgment and ridicule from my old friends, most of whom were still caught up in crime. I could already hear their laughs, the sly remarks. But despite all of that, I took the job anyway, and something unexpected happened—it changed my view of the world.

While sweeping the streets, I started noticing things I'd never paid attention to before. Simple things, ordinary things. I'd see parents walking their kids to school in the mornings. Both parents, together, smiling, sober, and well-dressed. It might sound unremarkable, but where I grew up, fathers were often absent, and mothers were worn out, angry, or hungover from the night before. Seeing these families made me wonder: was this what life could look like?

Then, on my lunch breaks, I'd sit in the park and watch joggers pass by. They didn't just run by without a care; they'd stop to pick up litter and put it in the bin. Someone else's rubbish—just picked up and dealt with as if it were their own responsibility. It was such a stark contrast to the estate where I grew up, where even picking up your *own* rubbish was a rarity. These small acts of care, of taking responsibility for the shared spaces we live in, left me feeling something I hadn't experienced in years—hope.

The moment that really hit me, though, was at Kingston train station. Every morning, I'd see the same homeless people sitting there, asking for change. And every morning, I'd see men and women in sharp suits, clearly heading to high-powered jobs in the city, stopping to offer them money, food, coffee, even cigarettes. These were the same kinds of people I had judged all my life—people with money, people with opportunities I felt I'd never have. Yet here they were, showing kindness and compassion to those society often overlooks.

These experiences started to change me. They helped me realize the world wasn't as cold and cruel as I had always believed. For the first time, I started to feel that maybe the world *was* a friendly place.

I think about Albert Einstein's quote often: "What is the most important question you can ask?" He answered, "Is the world a friendly place?" Because if you believe the world is friendly, you will build bridges of understanding. And I could see it now—these small, everyday moments of kindness were the bridges. They didn't erase the challenges of my past or fix everything that was broken, but they softened the edges of my fear and distrust.

This shift in perspective was a turning point for me. When I started to see the world as a friendlier place, I also started to feel safer. And when I felt safer, I was able to take a risk I'd never dared to before—I began reaching out for help.

Here's the thing: safety doesn't have to come all at once. It doesn't have to be built in giant, sweeping gestures. Sometimes it begins with something as small as noticing acts of kindness, letting them chip away at the walls you've built to protect yourself.

If you're in a place where the world feels unsafe, try looking for these small moments. A stranger's smile. Someone holding a door open. A jogger picking up litter. A person stopping to help someone who needs it. These are signs that the world isn't as cruel as it might seem, and that change is possible, even for someone like me.

And if you're already one of these people—the ones who pick up litter, who give their change to the homeless, who smile at strangers—you're doing more than you might realize. You're creating bridges. You're making the world feel safer for someone like me, someone who's still trying to believe in a friendlier world.

Kindness, even in the smallest acts, has the power to transform lives. It transformed mine. So, as you go about your day, remember this: your small act of kindness could be the spark that helps someone else take their first step toward healing, toward change, toward believing that the world is, after all, a friendly place.

AN INVITATION TO SEEK TRUE SAFETY

It's hard to know where to find safety these days. The places we once turned to—churches, gyms, community spaces—often feel like shadows of what they were meant to be.

Places of workship, for many, have become symbols of harm in- stead of sanctuary. Stories of abuse, corruption, and exclusion have drowned out the solace they were supposed to provide. It's heartbreaking because, for some, these places were their last hope for peace.

Gyms, spaces meant for connection and growth, often feel like arenas of competition. Mirrors and egos dominate, with people more focused on how they look than how they feel. Even martial arts gyms, places that should teach humility and discipline, can turn into battlegrounds of pride and bravado, where everyone is trying to prove they're the toughest in the room.

Then there's the self-development world. I've been walking this path since 2007, and I've seen it all—the promises of transformation, the beautifully marketed retreats and workshops. But too often, they feel like performances. The same people who were the "cool kids" in school have traded their uniforms for flowing robes, beads, and feathers, now parading as shamans or gurus, speaking in hushed tones and spiritual buzzwords.

But behind the polished veneer, you can feel it—the lack of depth, the absence of true authenticity. And that's what so many of us crave: something real, something genuine. Instead, you leave feeling more alone than ever, even in a room full of people.

Maybe it's because we've been burned too many times—by promises that fell flat, by systems that said they cared but didn't. Maybe it's because, deep down, we've stopped believing that real safety exists.

Or maybe it's because we've developed a sense for authenticity. When you've spent your life observing people's true motives, you learn to spot what's real and what isn't. You can feel when someone's words don't match their energy, when their compassion feels rehearsed, not lived. It's a skill born from survival, but it makes it even harder to trust and feel safe in spaces that are supposed to foster healing.

I understand this because I've been there. I've walked into rooms full of promises, hoping to feel safe, only to leave feeling more lost than when I arrived. It's a painful reality, but it's one we need to acknowledge.

The truth is, real safety is rare, but it is possible. I've seen it. I've felt it.

For me, the first flicker of safety came at nineteen years old, as a street sweeper in Kingston upon Thames. My life at that time was raw and chaotic, but something changed as I witnessed small acts of kindness—parents walking their children to school, joggers picking up litter, commuters offering food or money to homeless people. These moments softened something inside me, showing me that compassion and connection still existed. For the first time in years, I felt a tiny spark of safety within myself.

Later, at 25, I found safety with others in a small church on the Antrim Road in Belfast. I walked into an AA meeting full of Irish alcoholics and for the first time in years, I felt seen and understood. That feeling of safety, first found within myself and then with others, became the foundation I needed to start changing my life.

Safety isn't just about physical spaces or the right words—it's a feeling. It's in the way someone looks at you and says, "I've been there too." It's in their honesty, their humility, and their willingness to show their vulnerability.

Safety is something you can seek out, and it's something you can be for someone else. You don't need all the answers. You don't need to rescue anyone or offer magic solutions. Just listen. Really listen. Share your truth when it's needed—not to fix, but to connect.

For me, safety began in witnessing those small acts of kindness on the streets of Kingston Upon Thames and deepened in that church in North Belfast. It came from the lived experiences, stories, and willingness of others to say, "You're not alone."

I believe change is possible—not just for individuals like me, but for our systems, our communities, and our world. And if you're reading this, I want to encourage you: seek out safety. Not in titles or spiritual buzzwords, not in polished performances, but in the truth you see in someone's eyes.

Find safety by looking for the good in the world. Look for the random acts of kindness that often go unnoticed but are all around us. Look for the good people—they are out there, trust me. They may not be loud or seeking attention, but they exist in the quiet corners, doing the work, offering connection, and reminding us that safety and goodness are real.

Safety is the foundation for everything that follows. It's what makes the next step—awareness—possible. As we move into Chapter 2, we'll explore what it means to turn inward, to shine a light on the patterns and beliefs that have shaped us, and to begin understanding ourselves in a new way.

Because sometimes, safety comes from the people you least expect, in places you never imagined. Where will it come from for you?

CHAPTER 2
AWARENESS

"Our past will always be part of us, but the goal isn't to erase it. It's to understand it and not let it define who we are now."

Now that we've arrived at a place of safety, we can begin to gently shine the light of awareness onto the painful moments of our past. Safety is the foundation that makes this possible. Without it, even the thought of revisiting our pain can feel overwhelming, threatening to pull us back into the darkness of old survival mechanisms—the very ones that once gave us a false sense of safety.

When I first got sober in 2007, I thought life would magically get better. I imagined that putting the drink down would fix everything. I pictured myself waking up full of energy and hope, ready to rebuild my life. But the reality of sobriety hit me like a freight train.

While others around me in early recovery seemed to be riding a wave of positivity, I was drowning. I was unemployed, in debt, and feeling suicidal. The weight of my past mistakes and the reality of my present circumstances felt unbearable. For years, I had numbed myself with alcohol, and now that it was gone, there was nothing between me and the rawness of my pain.

One night in December 2007, I went to an AA meeting at the Braid Valley Hospital in Ballymena. It was bitterly cold, the kind of night where the frost on the car windscreens glistened under the streetlights. I arrived early, standing in the car park, smoking a cigarette to calm my nerves—a habit I had back then during those early, raw days of recovery.

I felt lost, unsure why I was even there. The weight of everything I needed to fix seemed overwhelming, and I had no idea where to start.

Colly, one of the old-timers, approached me. He was cheerful, with a warmth that didn't make sense to me at the time. He'd been sober for over 20 years, and I remember thinking, *How can someone go that long without a drink and still be so happy?*

He walked up to me with his hands tucked into his coat, nodded, and asked, "How are you, Michael?"

I hesitated but decided to be honest. "Not great," I admitted. "I'm feeling depressed. Powerless. There's so much I need to change, and I don't know where to start."

Colly listened without interrupting, his kind eyes fixed on me. Then, with a small smile, he said, "Michael, the good news about getting sober is that you get your feelings back. And the bad news is… you get your feelings back."

I stared at him, confused. Feelings? What did feelings have to do with anything? I nodded politely but thought, *What is this old fella talking about?*

As Colly walked inside, I stayed out in the car park, the cold biting through my jacket. I stood there in the silence, smoking, trying to make sense of what he had said. And then, it hit me.

Maybe this is why I drank.

Maybe I drank so I didn't have to feel what I was feeling right now.

That realization knocked the wind out of me. It was like a door had cracked open, letting in a sliver of light. If this was how I truly felt sober—crushed, hopeless, raw—then I needed to understand why. I needed to figure out if I had always felt this way or if this feeling had started somewhere else in my life.

That conversation with Colly in the cold December air was the beginning of my journey into awareness. It wasn't a sudden epiphany or a miraculous transformation—it was messy, uncomfortable, and deeply painful. But it was real.

Colly's words didn't give me answers, but they gave me something I hadn't had in years: curiosity. And that curiosity gave me a reason to look deeper.

Awareness isn't easy. It doesn't always feel like a gift when it arrives. Sometimes, it feels like a curse. For me, it came wrapped in regret, shame, and a sense of hopelessness. But it also came with a flicker of possibility—the idea that if I could understand these feelings, maybe I could begin to change them.

That moment outside the Braid Valley Hospital didn't solve everything. It didn't magically make life easier. But it was the start of something. It gave me the first glimpse of what lay beneath my drinking, and it set me on a path to uncovering the truth about myself.

Awareness isn't about having all the answers. Sometimes, it brings more questions than clarity. But those questions are a gift because they give us something to work with. They shine a light into the darkness and remind us that healing is possible, one step at a time.

And for me, it all started with a cheerful old Irishman named Colly, who taught me one of the hardest truths about sobriety: the good news is, you get your feelings back. And the bad news is, you get your feelings back.

Awareness can't happen without safety. It's only when we feel secure—when we trust we won't be overwhelmed— that we can look back with honesty and even a little courage to examine what we've endured and what we've lost. Without that foundation of safety, facing the past can push us deeper into survival patterns—numbing, denying, or avoiding. Safety creates the space where awareness can emerge, without fear of being consumed by it.

For me, that awareness came at the exact right place and time. I was standing outside the Braid Valley Hospital in Ballymena on a cold December night in 2007, smoking a cigarette before walking into an AA meeting. I was about to step into a room full of people I felt safe with—people who wouldn't judge me, people who had walked the same path. That moment of safety, of knowing I wasn't alone, gave me the courage to begin asking the hard questions.

For so many of us, this journey means facing the hurt we've carried, the broken dreams, and the innocence we lost along the way. It's about grieving the things that were taken from us and the parts of ourselves we sacrificed just to survive. Maybe it's the spark that dimmed, the hope that went quiet, or the belief in something better that got lost in the chaos.

In the past, these memories might have felt too raw, too overwhelming to confront. So we buried them deep, thinking that would protect us. But when we find stability—when we feel safe—those buried parts start to surface. Not to pull us back into pain, but to give us a chance to reclaim what we thought was gone forever.

Awareness isn't about reliving the past or letting it define us. It's about looking back with compassion, understanding that our pain doesn't determine our worth or dictate our future. It's about shining a gentle light on what happened, giving ourselves permission to grieve, to honour what we endured, and to begin releasing the burdens we've carried for far too long.

For me, awareness didn't arrive in a single moment. It crept in slowly, like the morning sunrise—gentle, steady, but undeniable. It started when I allowed myself to sit with my pain, to really see it, and to begin asking the hard questions: *Have I always felt like this when I'm sober? If not then when did I start feeling this way? What's the reason I'm feeling this way?*

Each memory that surfaced brought grief, but it also brought relief. Relief in finally feeling what I'd been avoiding for years. Relief in realizing I didn't have to carry it alone. And with every step, I began to reclaim the pieces of myself I thought were lost forever.

This is the work of awareness—to see clearly, to honour what was, and to give ourselves the space to heal. It's not easy. It's messy, painful, and sometimes it feels like too much. But it's essential. Without awareness, we stay stuck, repeating cycles of pain and avoidance. But with it, we can begin to rewrite our story.

Awareness showed me that healing is possible, that I could rebuild a life rooted in hope instead of hurt. And it can show you the same. It's not about fixing the past—it's about reclaiming your present and finding peace within yourself.

The journey of awareness begins here. And with it, the possibility of a brighter, more hopeful future.

BECOMING AWARE OF WHY WE SUPPRESS EMOTIONS

Looking back, I can see now that suppressing emotions wasn't a conscious choice—it was something I learned, a survival mechanism shaped by the world around me. On Ivybridge Estate in Isleworth, where I grew up as a child, emotions like sadness or fear were seen as weaknesses. Showing weakness wasn't just frowned upon—it was dangerous. To survive, I buried those feelings deep, never realizing the long-term cost of keeping them locked away.

One memory stands out vividly—a moment that helped cement the belief that emotions were liabilities, never to be shared.

It was a warm summer evening in 1990, and the estate was alive with the sounds of kids playing. The golden light of the setting sun bathed everything in a soft glow, making even the harsh edges of the estate feel, for a moment, like something out of a picture book. My friends and I were playing outside, lost in the simple joys of childhood—the kind of carefree laughter that feels infinite when you're young.

Then, the tone shifted. One of the older boys, looking over at Darren, broke the rhythm with a heavy question. "How you holding up, mate? With your mum and all?"

Darren's mum had died a few weeks earlier, another life claimed by the grip of addiction. Darren had been the one to find her that morning, slumped lifeless at the kitchen table while he came down for breakfast. It was the kind of tragedy none of us really understood at the time, but even as kids, we knew it was heavy.

The words hung in the air, and the world around us seemed to stop.

Darren froze. His face crumpled, and before he could even respond, the tears came. Not small, quiet tears, but big, heaving sobs that seemed to come from somewhere so deep it scared the rest of us. His pain was raw and exposed, and we didn't know what to do with it.

We were just boys. Boys raised in a world where crying wasn't allowed, where "big boys don't cry" was drilled into us before we could even understand what it meant. Darren's grief was too much—too real. I remember looking around at my friends, hoping someone would step forward, say something, do *anything* to ease the moment. But no one did.

We just stood there, frozen, watching Darren cry.

I remember feeling trapped in that moment, like time had slowed down and all I could do was watch. I wanted to comfort him, but the truth is, I didn't know how. None of us did. We were too young, too scared, too steeped in the rules of our world—the rules that said emotions like his had no place here.

Eventually, Darren's nan called him in for dinner, her voice cutting through the tension like a lifeline pulling him to safety. Darren wiped his face and turned to leave, his small shoulders slumped under the weight of his grief. As he walked away, the air around us shifted, and we all exhaled at once, a collective release of the pressure his tears had placed on us.

Then one of the older boys muttered, "Shit, man, I think Darren's lost it."

That sentence hit me harder than anything else that happened that day. In that moment, I made it mean something that would shape my life for years to come: sadness and vulnerability weren't welcome here. If I ever let myself cry, if I ever showed my fear or pain, I might end up like Darren—judged, dismissed, and left to carry my grief alone.

I didn't realize it at the time, but that moment planted a seed deep inside me. At eight years old, I decided that my sadness was something to hide, a part of myself that needed to be buried if I wanted to stay safe. Vulnerability wasn't just dangerous—it was a liability, one that could cost me everything.

And so, I locked it away.

I became an expert at pushing my feelings down, at pretending they didn't exist. I wore the mask of the tough kid, the one who didn't care, who didn't cry, who didn't feel. But inside, that little boy was still there, holding his sadness, carrying the weight of a world that told him he wasn't allowed to feel.

It wasn't until years later, when I began my journey into recovery, that I realized the price I had paid for burying my emotions. That day on the estate, I learned to survive by shutting down a part of myself. But survival isn't the same as living, and the cost of hiding that little boy's pain was far greater than I could have understood back then.

Maybe you've had a moment like this too. A time when you saw someone else's pain and played it down—not out of cruelty, but because their emotions brought up feelings you weren't ready to face in yourself. Or maybe you've been the one dismissed, your vulnerability met with discomfort or silence, leaving you feeling more alone than ever.

Suppressing emotions might feel like the safer option, but here's the truth: it doesn't make the pain go away. It hides it, stores it deep where it festers, shaping our behaviour in ways we don't even realize.

You might be asking yourself, *Why is it so important to recognize how we suppress emotions?* The answer is simple:

because awareness is the first step to breaking the pattern. When we understand where our suppression comes from, we can begin to undo it.

For me, that awareness didn't come until much later. But when I look back, I can see it so clearly now—an eight-year-old boy, trying to protect himself the only way he knew how.

If you're reading this and it resonates with you, I want you to know that healing begins with awareness. It starts with looking at the moments that taught us to hide our emotions and asking ourselves if those lessons are still serving us today.

For me, it was that summer evening on the estate, watching Darren cry and making a decision I didn't even know I was making. For you, it might be something else. But wherever it started, the awareness that comes with looking back is where the healing begins.

And it's never too late to start.

THE COST OF SUPPRESSING EMOTIONS: UNDERSTANDING THE SCIENCE

I'm not a scientist or a researcher, but when I first came across the science behind suppressed emotions, it hit me like a bolt of clarity. It wasn't just me. All those things I'd felt and experienced had a name, a reason, a connection to something bigger. I realized that the patterns I'd lived—the survival mechanisms, the struggles—were deeply rooted in how our brains and bodies respond to pain and trauma. That's why I like to back up what I'm saying with research.

Not because I'm an expert, but because it helps me show you that these struggles aren't isolated, and they're not yours to carry alone. This is shared human experience, and together, maybe we can start evolving how we approach these issues as a society.

1. The Impact on the Brain

Trauma changes the brain. Research shows that prolonged exposure to stress and unprocessed trauma can physically alter its structure, particularly in three key areas: the amygdala, hippocampus, and prefrontal cortex.

The amygdala, which processes fear and emotional responses, becomes hyperactive. This makes us more reactive to perceived threats, even when there's no real danger. It's like the alarm system in your brain gets stuck on overdrive. Meanwhile, the hippocampus, responsible for memory, can shrink. This affects our ability to process new experiences without constantly filtering them through the lens of past pain. Then there's the prefrontal cortex—the part of the brain that helps with rational thinking and decision-making. Under stress, it becomes less active, making us more impulsive and prone to destructive choices.

What's clear is that the emotions we suppress don't just go away. They linger, shaping our brains and influencing how we respond to the world. The first step to breaking this cycle is awareness—learning to recognize these reactions so we can begin the work of rewiring them.

2. The Impact on Physical Health

The mind-body connection is powerful, and unresolved trauma doesn't just affect the mind—it also takes a toll on the body. Studies have shown that suppressed emotions are linked to a range of health issues, including cardiovascular disease, chronic pain, digestive disorders, and autoimmune conditions.

Why does this happen? When we suppress emotions, it creates stress within the body, triggering inflammation and weakening the immune system. Think of it like holding a beach ball underwater: it takes effort, and that effort creates tension. Over time, the body pays the price. Simply put, when we bury our pain, it doesn't disappear. It finds other ways to make itself known.

3. The Impact on Productivity and Relationships

Suppressed emotions don't just stay inside—they spill over into every aspect of our lives, including our work and relationships.

When we carry unresolved pain, it clouds our ability to focus and stay present, making it harder to be productive or engaged. In relationships, suppressed trauma often shows up as irritability, impatience, or emotional shutdown. We might withdraw from those closest to us, afraid that showing our true selves will lead to rejection or ridicule.

But there's hope. Awareness can help us recognize these patterns and begin to choose differently. It gives us the chance to respond with connection instead of isolation, to show up fully in our work and relationships without being held back by unprocessed emotions.

I'm sharing this with you not because I've mastered it all or because I'm some kind of expert. I share it because when I learned about the science behind emotions and trauma, it gave me a way to make sense of what I'd been through. It reminded me that I wasn't broken or alone—that there's a reason these things happen, and that they can be changed.

AWARENESS OF HOW WE ESCAPE

For years, I didn't realize I was numbing myself. It wasn't just the drugs or alcohol—though they played a massive part—it was in the little things too. Distractions became my refuge. I'd bury myself in anything to avoid those quiet moments when I might actually have to sit with how I was feeling.

Escapism doesn't always look like addiction in the obvious sense. It's not just about the bottle or the needle. Sometimes, it's scrolling through your phone until your thumbs hurt, binge-watching TV until the early hours, or throwing yourself into work so you don't have time to think. It's the countless ways we keep ourselves busy, convinced we're being productive, when really, we're just avoiding the truth.

The truth is, we all escape because it feels safer than feeling.

When I started drinking, it wasn't about the taste or the social side of it—it was about silencing everything inside me. That first drink wasn't just alcohol; it was relief. It turned down the volume on the sadness, dulled the sharp edges of fear, and, for a little while, made me believe I wasn't carrying the weight of my past. But the relief never lasted. By the time the buzz wore off, everything I was running from came flooding back, sometimes worse than before. So, I'd reach for another drink, and the cycle would begin again.

But it's not just substances we use to escape.

For some, it's relationships. Clinging to someone who makes you feel seen or loved, even if the relationship is toxic. For others, it's food, finding comfort in the temporary relief of a full stomach. Then there are those who chase achievement—throwing themselves into success or perfection, believing that if they just do enough, they can finally outrun the pain.

Escaping isn't weakness. It's survival.

We escape because the emotions feel too big, too overwhelming, too much. It's what we do when we don't know how to sit with the sadness, anger, or fear. It's a way to cope, a way to avoid being swallowed whole by what we're feeling.

But here's the thing about escapism: it doesn't just shield you from pain—it shields you from everything.

When we numb sadness, we numb joy. When we bury fear, we also bury connection. When we distract ourselves from the hard stuff, we miss out on the good stuff too. I didn't realize how much life I was missing because I was too busy trying not to feel.

Looking back, I can see now that awareness was my way out. When I finally stopped drinking, I began to see all the other ways I was escaping. It didn't happen overnight, but I started to recognize the patterns—the places I ran to when life felt too hard to face. And with that awareness came a choice: to keep escaping or to stop, sit with the discomfort, and begin to heal.

I won't pretend it's easy. Feeling everything you've buried is one of the hardest things you'll ever do. But it's also where freedom begins. Because when you stop running, you start living.

Maybe, in one way or another, we're all addicted to escaping. It might not look like addiction on the surface, but whether it's substances, screens, food, or work, the pattern is the same. We all have something we reach for when life feels too much. But the key isn't to fight the escape—it's to understand it.

When we become aware of the ways we escape, we can start to ask the bigger questions: *What ways do I escape difficult emotions? Are any of the ways I escape, damaging to me or my loved ones? Has any of my escaping behaviours cost me more than money, have they cost me friends, jobs, relationships, health, dignity, freedom?*

Awareness doesn't fix everything, but it shines a light on the path forward. It gives us a chance to choose something better. And for me, it's shown me that the life I was trying to escape from was never the problem—it was the life I hadn't yet allowed myself to build.

We don't have to keep running. We can stop, feel, and begin again. And when we do, we might just find a life that doesn't need escaping at all.

TAKING THE FIRST STEP TOWARD FEELING AGAIN

All of our feelings stem from four primary emotions: anger, sadness, fear, and joy. These are like the roots of a tree, anchoring the many branches of emotions that grow from them. Anxiety often stems from fear, just as frustration might originate from anger. When we start to recognize these roots, we can make sense of what we're feeling instead of being consumed by it.

But for me, reconnecting with emotions wasn't just disorienting—it was agonizing. I grew up in a world where feelings weren't something you dealt with; they were something you drowned. Both my parents used alcohol or drugs as their solution to everything.

So, when I stopped drinking, I had no idea how to feel. The idea of sitting with my emotions was foreign—painful, even. It felt like learning to walk all over again, except this time the ground was uneven, and I kept stumbling with every step.

I'll never forget the early years of my sobriety. Feeling emotions again was like standing in front of a tidal wave. After years of burying them to survive, they came crashing down all at once. Anger would surface so fiercely it left me shaking. Sadness would creep in, raw and heavy, and leave me questioning if I could handle it. Fear wrapped itself around me like a fog, convincing me I was destined to fail.

One Friday night stands out vividly—a night I'd always used to drink, a night I'd always relied on for escape. Fridays were for drowning the week's frustrations in the bottom of a pint glass. But this night was different. I was sober, alone at home, and the silence felt suffocating.

My girlfriend at the time had gone out with her friends for some drinks, and I started to reflect on all the bad in my life, how I was stuck in a job I hated, drowning in debt, and overwhelmed by a tidal wave of emotions I didn't know how to handle. I sat on the edge of my bed, my chest tight with fear and anger, my head spinning with doubts. The sadness was heavy and raw, the anger came in sharp bursts, and the fear wrapped itself around me, whispering that I'd never get through this.

The temptation to escape was strong. I knew how to make it all stop. A drink would have taken the edge off, dulled the pain, made it all feel a little more bearable—at least for a while. But deep down, I knew I couldn't go back. Not if I truly wanted to change.

That night, I felt completely stuck. The feelings I'd buried for years were crashing over me, and I didn't know how to keep my head above water. For so long, my answer to everything—stress, anger, even joy—had been alcohol. Without it, I was left with nothing but raw, unfiltered emotion, and it was terrifying.

I picked up my phone and called Sean, my AA sponsor. He was the one person I knew I could trust with how I was feeling. When he answered, I didn't hold back. I told him everything—how much I hated my job, how scared I was about my debt, how lonely and powerless I felt. Sean listened without interrupting, without judgment, and somehow, just saying the words out loud eased the pressure in my chest.

He didn't offer quick fixes or tell me it would all be okay. He didn't try to solve my problems. He just reminded me to take it one step at a time. His calm, steady voice was like a lifeline, pulling me back from the edge.

That Friday night taught me something I hadn't fully understood before: learning to feel again isn't just hard—it's brutal. It's like learning to walk after years of being in a cast. Every step hurts, and sometimes you fall. But each time you pick yourself back up, you get a little stronger.

In the early days of my sobriety, reconnecting with my emotions felt like standing in front of a tidal wave. After years of burying them to survive, they came crashing down all at once. Anger would surface so fiercely it left me shaking. Sadness crept in, heavy and raw, making me question whether I could handle it. Fear convinced me I was destined to fail.

But that night, I didn't numb myself. Instead, I leaned on the safety I'd built—the pillars that kept me grounded when I felt like I was falling apart. Sean and other elders in AA, who helped me unpack the roots of my anger and fear, reminding me that my emotions weren't enemies but signposts pointing toward healing. And my AA friends, who sat with me three times a week in those rooms, nodding in understanding as I shared things I'd buried for years.

Every time I spoke, it felt like letting out a deep breath I hadn't realized I was holding. Their stories of pain and progress reminded me I wasn't alone. Those connections gave me the courage to sit with my emotions a little longer, to let them rise without letting them take over.

If you're reconnecting with your emotions for the first time, know this: you don't have to do it alone. The safety you've built—whether it's a trusted friend, a mentor, or a community—is there to catch you. And those feelings, as overwhelming as they might seem, aren't your enemies. They're your guides, pointing you toward the life you're working to create.

Feeling again isn't easy. It's messy, and it hurts. But on the other side of the pain is freedom. And that freedom is worth every step, every stumble, and every wave of emotion you allow yourself to face.

THE 5-SECOND RULE

I'll never forget the first time I heard about the 5-second rule. It was 2008, and I was a year sober, living back in Isleworth, trying to rebuild my life. Everything felt raw—emotions, relationships, and the simple task of getting through the day without letting my anger consume me. I was learning how to stay out of trouble, which, for me, meant finding new ways to deal with people who annoyed me.

This is what I learned growing up—when conflict arose, you didn't talk it out, you fought it out. Fists, aggression, or worse. That's how we resolved things in the world I came from. So now, trying to stay sober and out of trouble, I had to unlearn those instincts. Those first few years of sobriety were a process of replacing everything I'd known with tools to help me navigate life differently. One of those tools came from Eddie.

I was drawn to Eddie the moment I met him. He was like me, and that was rare in the rooms of AA back then. There weren't many young, sober men in South West London in 2008, and Eddie stood out. He was about my age, but he'd been sober a bit longer than I had. His life mirrored mine in so many ways—running the streets, getting into scrapes with the law—but somehow, Eddie had avoided prison. Among the AA members, he was a likeable chap, the kind of person everyone warmed to. He had this easy charm and a way of making you feel like you belonged, which was exactly what I needed back then.

One day, I asked Eddie for advice. I was frustrated and fed up, struggling to figure out how to deal with people who got under my skin. "What do you do," I said, "when someone's being an idiot? How do you stop yourself from reacting?"

He leaned in over his coffee mug and said, "Let me tell you a little trick I use, Michael. When you're in the heat of the moment, and you feel like the urge to react or smack someone in the mouth is about to take over, give yourself five seconds. Just five. Count them out loud if you have to."

I frowned at him, half-laughing. "Five seconds? What can five seconds possibly do when I'm ready to blow up?"

Eddie didn't argue. He just smiled that knowing smile of his—the one that said he'd been there and seen it all—and replied, "Try it."

At the time, I didn't think much of it. But a few days later, I found myself in one of those moments. Stuck in traffic, anger rising, fists clenched, and ready to blow a fuse. Eddie's words came back to me. "Five seconds."

I didn't want to, but I forced myself to stop and count. One. Two. Three. Four. Five.

In that tiny pause, something shifted. Those five seconds created a small window of awareness—a moment where I was reminded that it was okay. I didn't need to go into fight-or-flight mode. The heat of the moment cooled just enough for me to take a breath. My racing mind slowed down just enough to let reason slip in. I didn't lash out. I didn't let the anger win. Instead, I responded—calmly, thoughtfully, in a way that surprised even me.

Later, I replayed that moment in my mind. It seemed so small, so insignificant, but it had made all the difference. That brief pause gave me the space to notice the situation for what it was, to remind myself that I was safe, and to choose differently.

Over time, I started using the 5-second rule more and more. When sadness crept in and I wanted to numb myself, I counted to five. When fear gripped me and made me want to run, I counted to five. Each time, those five seconds created a space where I could breathe, think, and respond instead of react.

The breaths I took in those moments were just as important. Before then, I never gave much thought to breathing, but I've learned how powerful it can be. It's not just about filling your lungs; it's about activating the part of your nervous system that says, *You're safe. You can slow down.* That breath, paired with those five seconds, became a tool I carried with me everywhere.

Months later, I told Eddie how much that simple practice had helped me. He didn't gloat or say, "I told you so." He just gave me that same knowing smile, as if to say, "I knew you'd figure it out."

Eddie's still sober today, still helping people find their way, and his words still echo in my mind whenever life throws me into the deep end.

So, if you ever find yourself on the edge—ready to react, tempted to numb, or overwhelmed by emotion—try it. Take five seconds. Breathe. Let that tiny pause remind you that it's okay, that you're safe, and that you don't have to let the moment take control. Trust me, those five seconds can change everything.

Surprisingly, years later, I came across the science behind this exact method. That tiny pause and those deep breaths activate the **parasympathetic nervous system**— the part of your body responsible for calming you down, reducing stress hormones, and telling your brain that you're safe. It interrupts the fight-or-flight response and gives your mind the clarity to choose a thoughtful response over an impulsive reaction. Eddie's little trick wasn't just practical—it was rooted in how we're wired as human beings. Those five seconds really do help reset your mind and body, and for me, they've made all the difference.

BODY SCANNING: RECONNECTING WITH YOUR EMOTIONS

One of the most effective ways I've learned to reconnect with my emotions is by first reconnecting with my body. For years, I had no idea how disconnected I'd become. I carried tension in my shoulders, tightness in my chest, I clenched my jaw and had knots in my stomach, but I never stopped to ask what they meant. It was like my body was screaming at me, but I wasn't listening.

That began to change when I was introduced to a simple practice called a body scan. At first, I'll be honest—it felt strange, even unnecessary. I'd sit there thinking, *What is this all about?* It was so peculiar to me, almost laughable. But what I didn't realize then was that I was adding tools to my toolbox.

Up until that point, my options had been so limited. If something hurt emotionally, I'd drink, distract, or escape. Not my fault—it was just what I'd been shown. But through these new practices, I was learning different ways to cope, to feel, to heal. And now I share this with you, hoping that some of it will land and become a part of your own journey.

The process of a body scan is simple, but its impact can be profound. Find a quiet space where you feel safe, sit or lie down, and close your eyes. Start by bringing your attention to your toes. Notice any sensations—tingling, warmth, numbness, or tension—and just observe. Then, slowly move your focus upward, through your feet, your legs, your stomach, your chest, all the way to the top of your head.

What I love about this practice is that it asks nothing of you except to notice. There's no need to fix or change anything. If you feel tension in your jaw or tightness in your stomach, let it be there. Simply observe it with curiosity, not judgment.

As you move through your body, start asking yourself: *What am I feeling? Where does this emotion live in my body?*

When I began asking these questions, it opened a door I didn't even know existed. I remember once feeling an overwhelming sense of anxiety. My stomach was knotted, my chest tight, and my breath shallow. As I scanned my body, I started to ask, *If this feeling had a colour, what would it be?* The answer came quickly—red. Angry, pulsing red. Then I asked, *Does it have a sound?* It did. A low, growling hum, like an engine stuck in gear.

And then came the big question: If this feeling had a voice, whose voice would it be?

That one stopped me in my tracks. It wasn't my voice. It was someone else's—a voice from my past, one I'd internalized without even realizing it. It was critical, dismissive, and loud. As I sat with it, I realized exactly whose voice it was: an old school teacher who used to humiliate me in front of the entire class because I couldn't get the words right. That voice had followed me all these years, living rent-free in my mind, convincing me that it was mine.

But here's the thing—through these exercises, I discovered the power of awareness. For years, I had believed that angry, critical voice belonged to me, but it didn't. The moment I recognized it for what it was, something shifted. The anger I'd been carrying wasn't aimed at me or even at the world—it was directed at that old teacher for what he had done. And in that moment, instead of being angry with myself, I felt something else: sadness and compassion for that little boy, for everything he had to navigate, for the pain he didn't deserve.

That awareness changed everything. Naming that voice was the first step in quieting it, and for the first time, I could begin replacing it with one that was kinder, more compassionate, and truly my own.

This is the power of body scanning. It helps you connect the dots between your physical sensations and your emotional world. Often, emotions we suppress don't just disappear—they find a home in our bodies, waiting to be acknowledged.

By observing instead of reacting, you create a space where those emotions can surface safely. You let your body feel seen, heard, and supported. And in that space, healing begins.

It's not always easy. Sometimes the sensations you uncover bring up memories or feelings you thought you'd buried for good. But the act of sitting with those sensations, of listening to your body's whispers, is an incredible act of self-compassion.

For me, body scanning became a tool to untangle the roots of my pain. It taught me to notice the knots in my stomach or the weight on my chest not as something to avoid, but as signposts guiding me toward what needed my attention.

And as I gave myself permission to feel, to observe, and to heal, I began to realize something powerful: our bodies hold more wisdom than we often give them credit for. They don't just carry our pain—they also carry the key to our healing.

But perhaps the most important thing I realized is that this process is like mining for data. Those early days of body scanning gave me invaluable insights into myself. What I found was that I was afraid—a lot. Afraid of the future, of the uncertainty that felt overwhelming. And I was sad—a deep, aching sadness. There were so many unshed tears, so much unacknowledged pain from my childhood.

I wasn't ready to deal with all those emotions yet, nor did I have the tools to fully process them. But the awareness of them—that was a giant leap toward healing. Because you can't fix what you're not aware of. And every time I scanned my body, every time I sat with those sensations, I was gathering information. I was learning about myself in a way I never had before.

This practice might feel strange at first—it did for me—but it's a powerful tool for reconnecting with yourself. And as you mine for your own data, as you uncover the fears, sadness, or even joy that's been waiting to be acknowledged, you take one step closer to healing. One step closer to freedom.

CHECKING IN

Sometimes the emotions we face feel like too much to carry on our own, and checking in with others walking a similar path can be a lifeline. For me, this has been one of the most valuable tools in my journey. I think back to Eddie, Sean, and Colly—three men who were pivotal in my early sobriety. They didn't try to rescue me, fix me, or tell me what to do. Instead, they shared what had worked for them, and most importantly, they listened. They really listened.

But here's the thing: I believe as human beings we've forgotten the ancient art of listening. So often, we're just waiting for the other person to finish speaking so we can jump in. Sometimes I sit in coffee shops and overhear conversations, and no one's even taking a breath—they're talking over the top of each other. It's like no one is really hearing anyone; they're just talking for the sake of it. Now, look, I get it—maybe that works for everyday chatter. But when it comes to real connection, I believe a greater level of awareness and understanding can only be found in active listening.

When you practice this, you start to notice something remarkable: people say a lot without even speaking. Body language, tone, and facial expressions communicate more than words ever could. Studies show that up to 93% of communication is nonverbal—your posture, gestures, and eye contact can convey so much. But if we're constantly talking, we miss it. We can't truly listen to what's being said—verbally or nonverbally—and that's where the real connection happens.

As human beings, we were created with two ears and one mouth, and I believe that happened for a reason: we should talk less and listen more. So, if someone reaches out to you, take the time to really hear them. Listen not just to their words, but to their pauses, their body language, the unspoken. And if you're struggling, don't be afraid to check in with someone who will truly hear you.

Take this forward with you: listen more, judge less, and practice the art of being present. When we do this, we create space for more understanding and awareness

EMBRACING AWARENESS AS A PATH TO FREEDOM

Awareness is the light that helps us see the patterns we've outgrown, the grief we've buried, and the strength within us to believe in a new way of living—one rooted in compassion, connection, and growth. It's the first real step toward freedom, and it's where the healing journey begins.

But let me be honest with you—this isn't easy. I'm asking you to do something that, in today's world, feels almost unnatural. We live in a time of constant distractions, where most people are glued to their phones, scrolling through endless feeds, numbing out, and avoiding what's really going on within them. Disconnection has become the norm, and awareness goes against the grain.

Awareness asks us to stop, to look inward, and to face what we've been avoiding. It's not about dredging up pain for the sake of it—it's about reclaiming your power from the things that have held you back. It's about understanding the beliefs and behaviours that no longer serve you and choosing a new path: a path of healing, growth, and living differently.

For me, awareness didn't come all at once. In the early days of sobriety, it started while sitting in my AA home group at the Braid Valley Hospital in Ballymena. I'd park myself in a chair, shut my mouth for once, and actually listen. It wasn't easy—me sitting still and quiet? A minor miracle. But as I listened to others share their stories, I started to hear bits that sounded a lot like mine. That's where the awareness began, in those moments of connection and relatability.

What made it work wasn't anything fancy. It wasn't about sitting with some expert who had all the answers. It was about being surrounded by people who'd been through it—fellow alcoholics who weren't trying to fix me or dazzle me with degrees. They just spoke their truth. And it was by using my ears, not my mouth, that I began to learn about myself. Turns out, when you stop talking long enough, you might actually hear something useful.

As Carl Jung said, *"Until you make the unconscious conscious, it will direct your life, and you will call it fate."* Awareness is how we take back control. It's how we stop living on autopilot and start creating a life that reflects who we truly are.

As you reflect on this chapter, take a moment to revisit the questions we asked earlier. Awareness isn't just for those who've experienced trauma—it's something useful for all of us. Now, ask yourself:

- What ways do I escape difficult emotions?

  Are any of the ways I escape damaging to me or my loved ones?

  Have my escaping behaviours ever cost me more than money? Have they cost me friends, jobs, relationships, health, dignity, or even my freedom?

I get it—these questions aren't exactly the fun kind you'd bring up over dinner. But they're worth asking. I spent a large part of my life escaping reality—numbing myself, running from emotions, and doing anything to avoid being present. And here I am, writing about practicing awareness and being fully present. The irony isn't lost on me, believe me.

But the truth is, awareness isn't just about noticing the world around you; it's about noticing everything within you too. It's the start of something bigger. Awareness isn't the final step—it's the beginning. It's the gateway to honesty, where you'll confront the truths that awareness reveals. And that's what we'll explore in the next chapter.

Honesty is the key that unlocks the door to freedom. It's where we begin to face not just what's happened to us, but how we've responded to it, how it's shaped our choices, and what we need to let go of.

So, as you prepare to move forward, know this: change is possible. With safety as your foundation and awareness as your guide, were already on the path to something better.

CHAPTER 3

HONESTY

"Honesty was the key that opened the door to a new life."

When it comes to healing—not just from trauma, but from any difficult experience—awareness takes us to the door, but honesty is the key that opens it. Once we've acknowledged the pain, the patterns, and the ways we've been held back, the next step is perhaps the hardest of all: honesty.

Honesty asks us to go deeper. It's not just about recognizing what has happened to us—it's about being truthful about how we've responded to it. It's admitting the ways we've tried to numb the pain, the destructive habits or behaviours we've leaned on to cope, and the times we've avoided the truth because it felt too overwhelming to face.

It's also about admitting where we've gone wrong. Where fear, pride, or even denial led us astray. Honesty challenges us to take responsibility—not to beat ourselves up, but to free ourselves. Because the truth, no matter how uncomfortable, is what sets us on the path to real freedom.

The likelihood is that most difficult life experiences—not just trauma—are born from someone's lack of honesty. A lie told with bad intentions, or a narrative dressed up as truth when it wasn't. Maybe it was the dishonesty of someone you loved or trusted, a betrayal that cut deep. Or perhaps it was a system, a government, or a history built on half-truths and omissions. Dishonesty has a way of weaving pain into the fabric of our lives, leaving us to navigate the fallout of choices we didn't make but still have to endure.

Being honest is hard, and let's be real: most of us aren't shown how to do it. In fact, we're often shown the opposite. Governments lie and pass the consequences on to someone else or leave before taking responsibility for their actions. Wars have been fought for what people believed was a good cause, only for the truth to come out later, revealing motives that were far from noble. The history we're taught in school is often sanitized or told through a narrow lens, ignoring the wider, more uncomfortable truths.

So, I get it. When you arrive at this stage of the journey, especially when we start talking about honesty, a big part of you might think, *No, screw this. I'm not doing it.* It's normal for resistance to come up—it's uncomfortable, even scary, to face truths we've avoided for so long.

That was my reaction, too.

I spent most of my childhood surrounded by lies. The people who were supposed to love and protect me—my primary caregivers—lied to me again and again. "I won't do that again." "I won't drink today." "I'm sorry, I'll never hurt you again." Each lie chipped away at my trust until I learned not to believe anyone, not even myself.

One moment stands out in particular. I was about twelve years old, and my mum would tell me she was just "popping to the shop." Every time she said it, I would look her in the eye and plead, *Make sure you don't drink, Mum. Make sure you come straight home.*

Then I'd wait.

I'd sit by the window, watching for her to return. The afternoon light would stretch into evening, the sky fading from blue to grey, and still, no sign of her. I can remember the ache in my chest, the anxiety building as the hours ticked by.

At some point, I stopped asking her not to drink. I stopped waiting by the window. I stopped believing the words she said. It wasn't a conscious decision—I just accepted that honesty wasn't something I could expect, even from my own mother. That was my reality.

So, when I got sober at 25 and was told that honesty had to become a cornerstone of my life, it felt impossible. How could I embrace honesty when I'd been raised in a world where lies were the norm?

Lies weren't just told in my home—they were woven into the fabric of the community I grew up in. Life wasn't about being honest; it was about survival. You learned to get by however you could. Scamming the welfare, stealing to make ends meet, spinning stories to keep the bailiffs at bay—it was all part of life. Honesty wasn't a luxury we could afford.

But the problem with lies—whether they come from others or from ourselves—is that they create walls. Walls between you and the people you love. Walls between you and the person you want to become. And those walls don't just keep others out—they trap you in.

Looking back now, I can see that this was the fork in the road where I got to choose my destiny. I could continue to hide, deny, and deflect—or I could face the truth head-on.

Here's the thing about growing up in a world where dishonesty is the norm: it's not just about the lies you tell others—it's about the lies you tell yourself. The lies that say, *I'm fine. It's not that bad. I don't need help.* Those lies are the hardest to face because they've become part of who you are.

Honesty feels dangerous because it threatens to unravel the story you've built to survive. But as hard as it is, honesty is the only way to freedom. As Brené Brown said, *"Choosing to be honest is the ultimate practice of self-love and respect."*

In my early recovery, I started to realize that honesty wasn't just about admitting the big things—it was about facing the small, everyday truths, too. Like admitting when I was scared. Admitting when I was angry. Admitting when I didn't have all the answers.

But let me be clear: this isn't easy, especially for people who grow up in poverty. When your day-to-day life is about survival, there's no time to sit with your emotions or reflect on your actions. You're too busy trying to make it to tomorrow. Admitting you've lied, or that you've hurt someone, feels like a luxury you can't afford.

And yet, without honesty, the cycles continue. The pain, the mistrust, the disconnection—it all gets passed down, generation after generation. That's why honesty is so important. It's not just about healing ourselves; it's about breaking the cycles that keep us trapped.

I wish I could tell you there's an easy way to be honest. There isn't. But I can tell you this: the freedom on the other side is worth it. When you take that first step—when you look yourself in the mirror and admit the truth, no matter how painful—it's like a weight you didn't even realize you were carrying is lifted.

Honesty was the key that opened the door to a new life for me. It wasn't a one-time thing—it's a practice, something I have to work at every day. But every time I choose honesty, I take another step toward the person I want to be.

And if you're reading this, I want you to know you can do the same. It's not easy, but it's worth it. The truth really will set you free.

THE LIES WE TELL OURSELVES

As a teenager in prison, I learned quickly that showing any weakness wasn't an option. No sadness about losing my freedom, no fear of who might walk into my cell next. You had to carry yourself like nothing could touch you, a constant mask of strength that you wore at all times. And the thing about wearing a mask is, if you keep it on long enough, you start to believe it's who you are. Looking back now, I honestly can't understand how teenage Michael managed to get through all of that.

The cell was tiny, barely enough room for the two of us, yet I had to live in there with strangers for months on end.

Eating together, sleeping a few feet apart, and yes—using the toilet in front of each other. Let me tell you, there was no cubicle, no little curtain for privacy. You'd sit on the loo while another man sat three feet away, pretending not to notice. And I'm there, telling myself, *This is fine. This is normal. This doesn't affect me.* But honestly, who was I kidding? It wasn't fine, it wasn't normal, and it absolutely affected me. But I couldn't admit that—not to myself and definitely not to anyone else.

That was the lie I told myself, over and over: *I'm strong. This doesn't phase me. Prison can't break me.* But the deeper, more damaging lie was the one beneath it all. By denying my feelings—fear, sadness, even shame—I was sending myself a dangerous message: *Your emotions don't matter. There's no room for your sadness. You can't be afraid. You just have to be strong.*

The worst part is, I believed it. I normalised what wasn't normal, because that was the only way I could survive. But when you spend years lying to yourself, those lies take root. They become part of your identity. I've seen the same thing with ex-military veterans I've worked with—pushing emotions down just to get the job done until the deployment was over, or telling themselves, *I'll deal with it later when I get home.* But later never comes, and all those buried feelings start leaking out in other ways.

For many ex-servicemen and women, they normalised what they saw and experienced because, in that environment, it *was* normal—for them. It wasn't until they began sharing their stories and saw the shocked reactions from others that they realised the reality of what they went through was far from normal.

But, like prison, the military is a hostile environment. Showing weakness or being vulnerable can make you a target. It can risk you becoming a victim—or, in some cases, cost you your life. So, you bury it all. You tell yourself you're fine. You act like nothing phases you. But those feelings don't just disappear. They linger, building up in the background, until one day they find a way to come out.

Then there was the lie I told myself growing up—and one I know my mum believed too. Coming from an Irish Traveller background, we convinced ourselves the world was against us. That because of who we were—our lack of education, the oppression of Travelling people, the invisible forces holding us back—we didn't stand a chance. We believed the odds were unfairly stacked against us, that life couldn't change. But now, I know that was another lie.

The truth? Believing the lies is easier. It's much harder to accept the truth: that I can change it all. I just need to get to work. Because if the problem is outside of me—if it's the world, the system, or other people—I'm powerless over it. But if the problem is me—my mindset, my beliefs—that's something I can control. That's something I can change.

The solution? It starts with getting honest. Honest about the lies we've told ourselves, why we told them, and how they've held us back. Those lies might have helped us survive once, but they don't serve us anymore. Facing the truth is uncomfortable, even painful, but it's the only way forward. It's about letting yourself feel all those emotions you've buried, admitting that they matter, and then taking responsibility for what comes next.

Because the truth is, you're not powerless. You're not stuck. You're not defined by the lies you once believed. The moment you decide to get honest with yourself, you take the first step toward the life you deserve. And trust me, it's worth it.

BREAKING THE SILENCE

Honesty isn't just about being truthful with yourself—it's about being truthful with others. It's the courage to let people see the real you, no matter how messy or imperfect that might feel.

For me, one of the most transformative and terrifying moments of my life came when I finally broke my silence about a secret I had carried for over 20 years. I was 26 years old, sitting in the living room of my sponsor, Sean.

Sean was an old Irish man, the kind of person whose presence made you feel instantly at ease. There was a calmness about him, a safety that was hard to put into words. His home reflected that same warmth—a clean and tidy bungalow in Ballymena, with a fireplace gently crackling in the background and shelves filled with spiritual and AA books. It was the kind of place that felt safe, a haven where nothing bad could touch you.

I sat across from Sean, my hands trembling as I tried to steady my breath. The air felt heavy, the weight of my secret pressing down on me. For over two decades, I had carried this pain, buried it deep, and let it fester in the darkest corners of my mind. And now, I was about to speak it aloud for the first time.

"My first… my first sexual experience," I began, my voice faltering. "It wasn't curiosity or consent. It was abuse. My uncle."

The words fell into the room like stones, heavy and raw. I couldn't look at Sean. I stared at the floor, bracing myself for the worst. My mind raced: *What if he doesn't believe me? What if he thinks I'm broken? What if he pulls away?*

But Sean didn't flinch.

He leaned forward, his voice steady and filled with compassion. "I'm sorry, Michael," he said softly. "No child should have to endure such a thing."

Then, after a brief pause, he reached out his hand and asked, "Do you want a hug?"

For a moment, I froze. I didn't know whether to trust the moment. I wasn't sure if I could let my guard down, if I could allow myself to be vulnerable enough to accept his comfort. But something in his tone, in the sincerity of his words, made me let out a deep, shaky breath—a breath I hadn't realized I'd been holding.

I stood up, and Sean wrapped his arms around me. His hug was steady and unassuming, a gesture that said, *You're safe here.*

I didn't cry. Not fully. I felt the deep sadness in my belly, a weight I had carried for so long, but at the time, I wasn't equipped to release it. Still, something shifted in that moment. Something cracked open, just a little.

For so many years, I had carried the shame and pain of that secret alone. I had convinced myself that if anyone knew, they would see me as tainted, as damaged, as unworthy. But in that room, with Sean's steady presence and his simple act of kindness, I realized that my pain didn't make me unworthy—it made me human.

Breaking the silence didn't erase the trauma, and it didn't answer all the questions that lingered. But it was the beginning of something new. It was the first step toward healing.

For years, I had wrestled with the confusion the abuse had brought into my life, especially growing up in a community where being gay wasn't just frowned upon—it was outright rejected. I didn't know how to make sense of what had happened to me. Questions like *Does this make me gay? Am I broken? Am I unworthy of love?* haunted me well into adulthood.

But in Sean's bungalow, surrounded by his books and his quiet compassion, I began to understand that the shame I carried wasn't mine to hold. The silence I had lived in wasn't mine to keep.

Breaking the silence wasn't just about shedding light on my past—it was about inspiring others to do the same. Because healing can only begin when we dare to speak our truth. Trauma thrives in darkness, feeding off secrecy and shame. But the moment we name it, the moment we bring it into the light, it begins to lose its power.

That day in Sean's living room, with the faint crackle of the fireplace and the weight of my secret finally spoken, was one of the hardest and most important moments of my life. I didn't leave with all the answers, and I didn't walk away fully healed. But I walked away lighter, knowing that someone had heard me, believed me, and stood with me in my pain.

I share this story not because it's easy, but because I want you to know that no matter how heavy your burden feels, you don't have to carry it alone. Honesty is terrifying, I know. It asks you to take off your armour, to stand vulnerable in front of another person, and to trust that they won't turn away. But it's also the most liberating thing you can do.

Healing begins the moment we break the silence. And in breaking that silence, you may just find a strength you never knew you had. But it starts with finding that safe space—a person, a group, or even just one friend you feel safe with. Find your Sean, someone who will truly hear you without judgment, and take a chance.

It's not easy to open up, I know that. But the act of speaking your truth, even if it's just to one person, can be the first step toward freeing yourself from the weight you've been carrying. So, take a deep breath, find that person, and give yourself a chance.

HONESTY ABOUT ADDICTION

Everyone close to me—my girlfriend at the time, my mum, my younger brother Justin, and my sisters Sophie and Maria—told me the same thing: "You've got a drink problem." But I couldn't accept it.

I pushed back every time, convincing myself they didn't understand, that they were exaggerating. I had excuses for days. *I don't drink every day. I've never slept on a park bench. I don't wake up and drink first thing in the morning. So how can I have a problem?* I clung to those excuses like a shield, convincing myself I had it all under control.

Even when I finally walked into AA and met Sean—a man I instantly knew I could trust—I still couldn't fully admit it. Sean, with his classic Irish sense of humour and patience of a saint, tried gently getting through to my thick English skull. I'll never forget the way he said it: "Michael, if you walk like a duck and quack like a duck, well… you might be a duck." It was his subtle way of saying, *Mate, the signs are all there.* And somehow, even with his wit and wisdom, I still wasn't ready to hear it.

I sat there in those meetings, feeling safe and even relating to everyone's struggles. But still, I couldn't fully accept that I was one of them. Instead, I looked for all the differences and none of the similarities. *I've got a job. I don't drink every morning. I'm not as bad as them. And besides, I'm the youngest person here!* I told myself anything to set me apart, anything to hold onto the belief that I wasn't like them.

Because, let's be honest, the truth was harder to accept. If I admitted I was one of them, I'd have to do what they did—the twelve-step program. And that wasn't just about stopping drinking. It was about looking at me, really looking at myself, and working on me. And that terrified me. The idea of facing my own flaws, my own pain, my own part in the mess I'd made—it felt like too much. So instead, I clung to those differences, because it was easier than admitting the truth staring me in the face.

Yet here I am today, in full acceptance of that truth. I'm an alcoholic. And looking back, I can see how hard I fought against admitting it, how determined I was to hold onto the lies I told myself. But sometimes, it takes someone like Sean—someone who can gently nudge you in the right direction, even with a bit of humour—to help you see what's been right in front of you all along.

Denial is one of the many characteristics of addiction. It's what keeps us trapped, what stops us from facing the reality of how our lives are unravelling. For years, I convinced myself that alcohol wasn't the problem—it was my solution. It was how I coped with a difficult week at work, how I celebrated when my team won, how I let off steam, and how I forgot about all the pain I experienced in prison and as a child.

But here's the truth about addiction: as long as we rely on substances or behaviours to escape our pain, we remain stuck. Addiction is like putting a plaster over a deep wound. It might cover it for a while, but it constantly needs tending to, again and again. The wound never truly heals.

Sobriety is the first step toward addressing the deeper wounds beneath the addiction. It's not about judgment or moral failure—it's about creating the conditions for real healing. Getting sober doesn't mean the pain goes away immediately, but it allows you to finally start tending to the wound properly, to heal it permanently.

In my own journey, I spent years avoiding this reality. I told myself I could manage my drinking, that I wasn't like the "real" alcoholics. But deep down, I knew the truth: alcohol wasn't just a problem—it was my lifeline. And the problem with that lifeline is that it never actually solves anything. It just delays the pain, making it louder and harder to ignore every time it resurfaces.

Honesty about addiction is the only way to begin the process of real healing. This means acknowledging that you cannot fully move forward while continuing to rely on substances or behaviours to cope. It means embracing abstinence-based recovery, where sobriety becomes the foundation for everything else.

Research supports this approach. Studies show that long-term abstinence, coupled with structured recovery programs like AA or NA, leads to significantly higher rates of sustained recovery and emotional well-being. According to *Alcohol Research: Current Reviews*, those who actively participate in AA are not only more likely to remain sober but also report higher levels of life satisfaction and reduced emotional distress. This isn't just about stopping the behaviour—it's about creating a life where the need to escape no longer exists.

Without honesty about addiction, it's impossible to address the deeper wounds beneath it. You might try to heal in other ways—therapy, self-help books, personal growth workshops—but without abstinence, those efforts will only be surface-level. They'll act as temporary bandages, not the deep, transformative work that true healing requires.

This isn't easy. Addiction is often rooted in trauma, pain, and unmet needs. It's a way of surviving, of numbing the unbearable. But survival mode isn't living. And the first step to moving beyond survival is getting honest about what's keeping you stuck.

I'm a firm believer that you can't truly heal your trauma until you address the addiction. Sobriety gives you the clarity to look at your life for what it really is. It allows you to confront your past, grieve your losses, and reclaim the parts of yourself you thought were gone forever.

I know this because it worked for me. Sobriety didn't just save my life—it gave me a life.

So, if you're wondering if you have a problem with alcohol or drugs, let's take a moment of honesty. Ask yourself: Do I drink or use drugs when things are hard? When I've had a tough week? Do I drink to celebrate the good things—Christmas, birthdays, promotions at work? And here's the big one: How does it feel when you think about not drinking or using on any of those occasions? Does the idea make you uncomfortable? Do you feel like you'd be missing out?

Now, let's fast-forward the videotape five or ten years into the future. If you keep going the way you are, is this really the life you want? Picture it—are you the person who drank at every occasion, every high and low, or are you the one who was fully present for your loved ones? The one who could actually be there to support them when life got tough, not just sit in the corner nursing a drink?

And I know, I know—right now, it might feel like I'm poking an angry bear. You might be thinking, *Who does this guy think he is? Why did I even buy this book?* Maybe you want to slam it shut or even chuck it across the room. Believe me, I've been there. But let me say this: I care about you enough to risk annoying you. Because if these words bother you enough to stick with you—if they make you stop and think, *Hang on, is this really where I want to be in 5 years?*—then it's worth it.

You see, people like Sean, Colly, and Eddie did the same thing for me. They didn't sugarcoat it. They challenged me. They made me uncomfortable. And at the time, I hated it. I sat there thinking, *Who do they think they are?* But here's the thing—they weren't trying to tear me down. They cared enough to tell me the truth. They saw something in me I couldn't see in myself, and they pushed me to be better.

So now, I'm paying it forward. I'm asking you to take a good, hard look at your life and ask yourself: Is this where you want to stay? Because here's the truth, and it might sting a little—if you keep doing what you're doing, nothing's going to change. But if you're willing to take the first step, if you're willing to be honest with yourself, then everything can change.

You've got a choice. Be the person who shows up for their loved ones, fully present, or be the one who keeps reaching for the drink or the drugs to numb the highs and the lows. It's up to you. And trust me, one day you'll look back and thank yourself for choosing the better path.

GETTING HONEST ABOUT THE DAMAGE YOU'VE CAUSED

When I got sober, I committed to completing the twelve-step programme of recovery. Steps eight and nine are among the most difficult: making a list of the people you've harmed and being willing to make amends to them all, except when doing so would injure them or others.

I can't describe the fear I felt as I sat with that list, knowing I would have to face those people. The dread of rejection, the weight of shame, the guilt of knowing I'd caused real harm—it was overwhelming. And then there was the fear of physical confrontation. The thought that some of these people might not just reject me, but actually come at me, was terrifying.

But this level of honesty, as daunting as it was, offered something very unique. It wasn't just about owning up to the harm I'd caused—it was about taking full ownership of my actions, something no man in my family's history, on either my mother's or father's side, had ever done. It was about stepping into a truth I'd spent years avoiding. I had spent so long running from the damage I'd caused, numbing the regret, and burying the memories deep. But now, there was no hiding.

I stand here today as a man who faced every single one of them. A man who made amends to every person I hurt. It wasn't easy. Seeing the looks on their faces—the disappointment, the sadness, the hurt—was brutal. But it was also liberating. In those moments, I realised something that has stayed with me ever since: *I never want to be the person who causes that kind of harm again.*

One of the hardest parts of this journey is getting honest about the damage we've caused. When we carry unhealed wounds, we often respond to life from a place of hurt, distrust, and fear. And in doing so, we may inflict similar pain onto others, even without meaning to.

It's not easy to look at this honestly. You may not have been physically abusive, but perhaps you were emotionally abusive—cutting with your words, shutting people out, or manipulating situations to protect yourself. Maybe you neglected, used, or hurt people without fully understanding the harm you were causing. These behaviours often come from survival mode, reacting to the world with the only tools you knew at the time.

But this journey requires us to take responsibility. It means putting your hands up and saying, *I'm sorry.* Not as a way to erase what happened, but as a way to own your actions and commit to doing better moving forward. This is the work of clearing up your side of the street.

The twelve-step programme forced me to take a fearless and searching moral inventory of my life. I had to look at my actions with brutal honesty—the lies I told, the trust I broke, the people I hurt. But it wasn't just about acknowledging what I had done—it was about understanding why I did it.

Addiction had been my escape, my way of numbing the pain I didn't know how to face. But that escape came at a cost—not just to me, but to the people around me. That was the truth I had to confront: my actions had consequences, and my pain didn't justify the harm I caused.

Making amends isn't about seeking forgiveness or expecting a clean slate. The person you apologise to may not accept your apology, and that's okay. Because the purpose of making amends isn't about their reaction—it's about your willingness to take responsibility. It's about acknowledging the impact of your actions and showing up with humility and accountability.

But making amends isn't just about saying sorry—it's about what comes next. It's about changing your behaviour, committing to living differently, and working to heal the wounds that drove your actions in the first place.

I remember one amends that felt particularly heavy. I stood in front of someone I'd hurt deeply, someone who had trusted me and who I had betrayed in ways I'm still ashamed of. As I spoke, I saw the pain in their eyes, and it broke something in me. But it also brought clarity. For so long, I had told myself that I was beyond saving, that I was just a bad person. But standing there, I realised that I wasn't a bad man—I was a hurt man, acting out of pain and survival.

That moment changed everything. It wasn't about absolution—it was about transformation.

When we take ownership and make amends, we free ourselves from the weight of guilt and shame that's held us down for so long. It's not just about saying sorry—it's about stepping into a new way of living where we're no longer looking over our shoulder, waiting for the past to catch up with us. Taking ownership allows us to move forward—not as the person we once were, but as someone striving to live with integrity, humility, and compassion. It's about facing the truth head-on and finally finding the peace that comes from knowing we've done our part to make things right.

This process isn't perfect, and it won't always be easy. The fear, the guilt, the shame—they're all part of it. But so is the freedom that comes with it. Every act of accountability, every moment of honesty, brings you closer to the person you were always meant to be.

If you're carrying guilt for the harm you've caused, take a moment to reflect. Ask yourself: *What steps can I take to own it and make things right?* This isn't about perfection—it's about progress. Each step toward accountability is a step toward freedom, a step toward healing. And that journey, as difficult as it may be, is worth every single moment.

HONESTY: THE KEY THAT OPENS THE DOOR

Honesty was the key that opened the door to a new life for me. Without it, I'd still be trapped—caught in the lies I told myself, unable to move forward. We've journeyed through the first three stages of healing: finding safety, shining the light of awareness, and now, stepping into honesty. Each step builds upon the last, creating a foundation for true transformation.

To recap: In safety, we learned that healing begins in a space where we feel secure enough to let our guard down. Without this, no progress is possible. In awareness, we explored how to uncover the patterns we normalized, the pain we numbed, and the emotions we suppressed. Now, in this chapter, we've stepped into honesty, where we confront the reality of what happened to us, how it has shaped our lives, and the ways we've hurt others in the process.

But as you stand at this pivotal stage, resistance might bubble up. You might start questioning: *Do I really need to do all of this? Do I need to address my addiction? Change my behaviours? Make amends? Clear up the wreckage of my past?*

The answer is yes.

If you want to create a life of true meaning and purpose, you can't skip this part. There are no shortcuts, no stones left unturned. Healing requires that we face everything—every choice, every behaviour, every hurt we've caused—with honesty and integrity.

This isn't just about doing the work for yourself; it's about showing up fully for your family, your loved ones, and your community. It's about becoming someone they can count on, someone who doesn't look over their shoulder in shame or guilt, but stands tall, rooted in truth.

You might feel guilt creeping in—guilt for surviving your trauma when others didn't, guilt for making someone you love look bad by confronting the truth of your experiences. Or maybe denial starts whispering in your ear: *Was it really that bad? Am I exaggerating? Is my addiction truly an issue?*

Let me assure you, these doubts are normal. Trauma distorts our perception of reality, making us second-guess ourselves. But here's the truth: honesty isn't about judging or comparing your pain; it's about owning your story so that you can begin to heal.

The work of honesty is hard. It asks you to take responsibility for your life in ways that might feel overwhelming. But the freedom that comes from this level of integrity is worth every moment of discomfort. It's worth it because it allows you to create a life where you no longer have to hide, no longer have to carry the weight of guilt and shame.

This is where real healing begins—when we stop running, stop numbing, and stop pretending. When we step fully into our truth, we not only free ourselves, but we also show others that they can do the same. Honesty isn't just the key that opens the door; it's the path that leads to a life of purpose, meaning, and connection.

A PATH FORWARD

As we close this chapter, I want to take a moment with you to reflect on the profound importance of honesty in your journey. Honesty isn't just about acknowledging what happened—it's about giving yourself permission to feel the full weight of it and understanding how it has shaped you. Trauma and challenging life experiences leave a mark, and denying its impact only deepens the wound. True healing begins when we face the truth, no matter how painful or uncomfortable it may be.

Jordan Peterson said, *"The truth is something that burns—it burns off deadwood, and people don't like having their deadwood burnt off, often because they're 95% deadwood. But it's a good thing to burn it off because you're left with something real."* In this journey, honesty acts as that fire. It burns away the lies, illusions, and defences we've clung to in order to survive. What's left behind is your authentic self—the version of you that's ready to heal, grow, and move forward.

Let's be real: honesty isn't easy. It's raw, vulnerable, and often uncomfortable. But it's also liberating. When we face the truth, we give ourselves permission to grieve, to let go, and to begin rewriting our story. Honesty frees us from the cycle of avoidance and numbing that keeps us chained to the past.

Take a moment to reflect on these questions:

- What truths about my life am I still avoiding?
- What would it look like to let go of the guilt, shame, or denial that's keeping me stuck?
- How might embracing the truth set me free?
- Are there substances or bad habits I'm using to avoid discomfort or difficult emotions?
- What parts of my life feel out of alignment with who I really am?
- Am I being fully honest in my relationships—with my loved ones, my family, my friends, or even myself?
- How are my behaviours and bad habits affecting the people I care about most?
- If I were completely honest with myself, what would I need to change?

These aren't easy questions, but they're the ones that create space for growth. They're for anyone who wants to live more authentically and feel more connected to themselves and the people they love. Life has a way of piling on roles, habits, and expectations that pull us away from who we really are. These questions are about pausing, taking stock, and choosing to get real with yourself.

Maybe your struggles aren't rooted in trauma, but in the daily challenges of life—balancing work and family, navigating relationships, or figuring out who you are in the midst of it all. Honesty matters just as much here. It's not about comparing your pain to anyone else's; it's about allowing your truth to emerge, no matter what it looks like.

When we get honest with ourselves, we start to see the little ways we hold back in life. It could be a habit we know isn't serving us, a relationship we're afraid to address, or a dream we've buried out of fear. These moments of reflection are transformative. They help us realign with what truly matters and begin to live in a way that feels authentic and free.

Honesty is about asking yourself: *Am I living in a way that feels true to me? Am I showing up fully for myself and the people I love?* The answers won't always come easily, but they're worth exploring. Because when we let go of the small lies—the ones we tell ourselves to stay comfortable— we create space for something better. Something real.

This is your invitation to embrace honesty—not as a burden, but as a doorway to freedom. It's not about perfection; it's about making space for connection, healing, and growth.

In the next chapter, we'll take the next step: *Processing the Pain.* It's one of the hardest parts of the journey, but it's also the most transformative. Facing the truth prepares us to move through the pain, to feel it in all of its intensity, so we can finally move forward.

CHAPTER 4

PROCESSING THE PAIN

"We can't heal what we refuse to feel. Processing pain isn't about reliving the past—it's about releasing its hold on us."

Processing pain is a deeply personal journey, and no two paths look the same. I'm not a doctor or a therapist. I don't come to you with academic credentials or theories from a textbook. What I bring is something raw, something lived—experience forged in the fire of my own healing.

Since 2007, I've been on this path, and let me tell you, it has not been easy. It's been relentless at times. There have been moments of unimaginable pain, nights spent crying, screaming, raging, and feeling like I was being torn apart from the inside out. I've revisited every dark corner of my past, every trauma, every heartbreak. And there were many moments when I didn't think I could make it.

There were times I doubted whether I could even be repaired after all the damage I'd been through. I wondered if there was too much pain, too much brokenness, too many years lost to ever truly heal. And yet, here I am—a changed man, standing on the other side of it, proof that change is possible.

I remember one particular moment that shifted my understanding of pain and healing. I was sitting with a Lakota elder, a man whose wisdom ran deep, like the rivers of his ancestors. He shared a story with me about the buffalo—an animal central to the survival of the Lakota people, who once lived on the plains of North America.

He explained that the buffalo were vital to their way of life. Every part of the animal was used—nothing went to waste. But the Lakota didn't just rely on the buffalo for sustenance; they studied the buffalo's movements, its interactions, its way of surviving the harsh, unforgiving environment of the plains.

One of the most valuable lessons they learned came from watching how the buffalo faced storms. When the skies darkened, and the winds picked up, all the other animals would run for the hills, trying to escape the storm. But not the buffalo. The buffalo would come together, forming a protective circle with the young, the old, and the vulnerable placed safely in the middle. The strongest buffalo stood on the outside, and then—together—they would walk directly toward the storm.

While every other animal ran away, the buffalo faced the storm head-on.

The elder looked at me with steady eyes and said, "This is what I want you to learn, and this is what I want you to share: be like the buffalo. Don't run from the storm. Gather your strength, surround yourself with support, and walk straight into it. That's how you survive. That's how you grow."

That story has stayed with me ever since. And now, I share it with you.

What I'm asking of you isn't easy—it's to be brave like the buffalo. To turn and walk toward the storms in your life, to face the pain you've been running from. Because here's the truth: avoiding the storm doesn't make it disappear. It just keeps it looming on the horizon, waiting for you.

What you're about to read isn't conventional. These methods go against what many doctors or therapists might tell you. But this is my personal journey, and it worked for me. What I share in this chapter isn't theory—it's truth. It's the work I've done to grieve the innocence I lost as a boy, the years I spent locked away, and the dreams of a relationship with my father that never come true until the final years of his life.

This isn't about convincing you to follow my path. It's about showing you what worked for me in the hope that you might find something here that resonates. Something that gives you the courage to take the next step on your own journey.

This journey hasn't been a straight line for me. It's been full of ups and downs, setbacks and breakthroughs. There were days when the pain felt endless when the weight of revisiting my past seemed too much to bear. But I kept going, one step at a time.

I've sat in rooms filled with strangers, pouring my heart out when my throat felt like it might close from fear. I've stood in forests under open skies, screaming my rage into the wind. I've cried tears that seemed like they would never stop—tears of grief, of regret, of exhaustion. And I've found moments of peace I never thought I'd experience, moments of release when I let go of the weight I'd been carrying for decades.

This is what it looks like. It's messy, it's painful, and it's deeply, deeply human.

But here's the truth: as hard as this work is, it's worth it. Every tear, every scream, every moment when I wanted to give up brought me closer to freedom. Because with each release, I let go of a little more of the pain that had held me captive for so long.

Processing pain isn't about staying stuck in the past—it's about breaking free from it. It's about reclaiming your life, your identity, your power.

So, as you read this chapter, I ask you to be like the buffalo. Face your storm. Gather your strength. Know that while the journey is hard, you're not alone—and the peace waiting for you on the other side is worth every step.

PROCESSING THE PAIN

Once we've created safety, cultivated awareness, and embraced honesty, we come to the hardest and most necessary part of healing: processing the pain. It's a stage that many of us avoid for as long as possible because it requires us to face what we've spent years running from. But avoiding it only deepens the wound. The only way out of the pain is through it.

For me, this stage was the most confronting. There were days when I wanted to turn back, to numb myself with distractions, to convince myself that I didn't need to dig any deeper. But the truth was, the pain was already there, shaping every part of my life in ways I didn't fully understand. It affected my relationships, my choices, and my sense of self.

The personal price I paid for avoiding my pain was steep. In my intimate relationships, I struggled to let anyone too close. I'd built walls around my heart, born out of the fear that if someone got close, they would hurt me— just like everyone else who got close to me did when I was a child. My fear of being hurt became a barrier to true connection. Even with my wife in the early stages of our relationship, there were moments when I'd pull back emotionally, convinced that staying distant would keep me safe.

It wasn't just my intimate relationships that suffered. My relationships with men were equally strained. My abuser was a man, and the majority of my trauma from prison came at the hands of men. I struggled to trust them, to not see every man as a potential threat. I carried this suspicion into every interaction, whether it was a conversation with a stranger or working alongside men in my professional life. Deep down, I believed that men were secretly out to get me, to take advantage of my vulnerabilities.

This pain, left unprocessed, shaped my entire worldview. I walked through life on high alert, constantly bracing for betrayal or harm. I didn't realize how much it was costing me—how much joy, connection, and peace I was sacrificing just to keep the pain buried.

It wasn't until I stopped running and started feeling that I began to experience real change. Processing the pain wasn't just about confronting what had happened to me;

it was about confronting what it had done to me—how it had hardened me, shaped me, and held me back.

WHY WE AVOID PAIN

Pain is something we're biologically wired to avoid. Our nervous system is designed to protect us, to pull us away from danger—whether it's physical or emotional. But trauma is different. It doesn't just pass through us; it lodges itself in our bodies, stored in our nervous system like an unhealed wound. Suppressing it doesn't make it disappear—it festers. It shows up as anxiety, anger, depression, addiction, or even physical illness.

Dr. Bessel van der Kolk, author of *The Body Keeps the Score*, explains, *"Trauma is not just an event that took place in the past; it is also the imprint left by that experience on the mind, brain, and body."* Suppressing pain doesn't erase it; it embeds it deeper into our being, shaping how we see ourselves, how we interact with others, and how we experience the world.

Many of us were taught—directly or indirectly—to avoid our pain. Growing up on the Ivybridge Estate, I learned early that emotions like sadness or fear were dangerous. Vulnerability made you a target, and showing pain was seen as a sign of weakness. So, I buried it. But buried pain doesn't disappear—it waits, surfacing when you least expect it.

Maybe you can relate. Maybe you avoid your pain because it feels too overwhelming to confront. Perhaps you tell yourself you're too busy, that life doesn't allow time to sit with your feelings. Or maybe you're afraid of what you'll uncover if you open that door. You might even believe that addressing your pain means revisiting the people or places that hurt you, and that feels like too much to bear.

Whatever the reason, know this: you're not alone. Avoiding pain is a survival mechanism. It's how many of us cope when we don't have the tools or support to face what's inside.

For a long time, I didn't understand this about my own parents. Both my mum and dad came from traumatic childhoods. My father, addicted to drugs and violence, was carrying wounds I'll never fully understand. My mum, who grew up in care after being taken from her Traveller family, carried the weight of rejection and exclusion her entire life. They both turned to alcohol and, in my father's case, drugs to numb their pain.

For years, I was angry at them for their choices, for the chaos and hurt they brought into my life. But when I began to understand the impact of trauma and how it shapes our ability to cope, it allowed me to feel compassion for them. They weren't bad people—they were hurt people, just trying to survive in the only way they knew how.

Understanding this didn't excuse their behaviour, but it helped me make peace with it. It also helped me see how I had inherited some of the same patterns of avoidance. For me, it wasn't alcohol or drugs—it was distraction, anger, and shutting people out. But the root was the same: unprocessed pain, desperately looking for an escape.

The truth is, the pain we suppress isn't just affecting us—it's affecting our relationships, our choices, and our overall well-being. It seeps into every part of our lives, shaping how we love, how we trust, and how we show up in the world.

It's a hard truth to face, but there is hope. When we stop avoiding our pain and start processing it, we create space for healing and growth.

THE COST OF SUPPRESSION

The pain we suppress finds ways to express itself, often in destructive ways. It might show up as explosive anger, numbing behaviours, or unhealthy relationships. For me, it showed up as addiction. Drinking dulled the ache inside me, but it didn't heal it. In fact, it kept me from ever dealing with the root of my pain.

Over the years, I've met countless men in prison who acted out their unresolved trauma while under the influence. They went into what's often called "the red mist," losing themselves in rage or despair and hurting someone else in the process. For some, this resulted in a single moment of violence that changed the course of their lives forever. I've spoken with men who were carrying the scars of childhood abuse, abandonment, or war, and instead of addressing their pain, they let it fester until it erupted.

I've worked with men who, after surviving the trauma of warzones across the world, came home and created warzones in their own homes—among their wives, children, and loved ones. For others, the warzone is internal, a relentless battle playing out in their minds, leaving them trapped in cycles of guilt, shame, and destruction.

The links between trauma, suppressed emotions, and destructive behaviour are undeniable. According to research, people who experience trauma are far more likely to develop addictions, exhibit violent behaviour, or attempt to take their own lives. In fact, trauma is a significant risk factor for suicide. The World Health Organization estimates that nearly 700,000 people die by suicide every year globally, and studies show that a large proportion of these deaths are directly or indirectly linked to unresolved trauma.

The weight of suppressed pain doesn't just stay buried; it finds ways to seep out, impacting not just the individual but everyone around them. Processing that pain is like cleaning out a wound—it's messy, uncomfortable, and can feel unbearable at times. But without addressing it, the wound never heals; instead, it infects everything it touches.

HOW TO BEGIN PROCESSING THE PAIN

Processing the pain isn't easy—it asks for courage, vulnerability, and patience. But the rewards of doing this work are life-changing. It's only by facing and working through the pain that we can begin to heal the wounds it has left behind.

I truly believe that unless we go back and fully heal the wounds of our past, those wounds will continue to direct our lives and then be passed on to the next generation. They don't disappear on their own—they find their way into how we live, how we love, and how we raise our children. Someone has to be brave enough to face it, to break the cycle, and to choose healing.

Here are some practices that can help guide you through this transformative process.

GRIEVE WHAT WAS LOST

Healing is not a straight path. It twists and turns, often circling back to old wounds we thought were closed. For me, one of the most pivotal parts of my journey was learning to grieve—not just for the people I'd lost, but for the parts of myself that had been taken away, the years that had been stolen, and the dreams that would never come true.

Grief is often misunderstood. It's not just sadness over a loved one's passing. It's the ache of what could have been, the weight of unspoken words, and the pain of letting go of a fantasy that you've held onto for far too long. I had to grieve the innocence that was taken from me as a child, the time I lost locked away in a prison cell, and, later, the hope that one day my father would become the man I needed him to be.

It was a quiet night in Isleworth. The kind of night where everything seems still, but your mind won't stop. I was five years sober, sitting in the back garden at my old wooden table, a fire pit glowing in front of me. The warmth of the fire couldn't touch the cold dread I felt inside. I'd spent years avoiding my past, burying the pain, the anger, and the shame. But for some reason, that night felt different. It felt like it was time.

I picked up a piece of paper and a pen and stared at the blank page for what felt like forever. The words didn't come easily at first. I wasn't even sure where to start. But then, like a dam breaking, everything poured out.

I wrote to the people who had let me down, the ones who were supposed to love and protect me but didn't. I wrote to the friends who disappeared when life got hard, the ones who turned their backs on me when I needed them most. I wrote about the fights in prison as a teenager, the fear of being completely alone, and the anger I'd carried because of it. I wrote about the racism and bullying I faced for being one of the only white kids who stood up for himself, the constant need to prove I wasn't an easy target. That need to fight back—to survive—left its mark on me, long after the prison doors had closed behind me.

Then I wrote about my dad. I didn't hold back. The anger I felt toward him poured onto the page—anger for not being there when I needed him, for not stepping in to protect me when life got too much. I wrote about the times I wished he had been stronger, wished he had shown up for me in a way that could have changed everything.

But as I sat there, the fire crackling softly in front of me, something else started to surface. I found myself thinking about his dad—my grandfather. I thought about how he came back from World War II with undiagnosed PTSD and brought the war home with him. For my dad, home wasn't a safe place; it was a warzone. And then, when I came into the world, that warzone became mine too.

I pictured my granddad, struggling with demons he didn't have the tools to fight, and my dad, growing up in that chaos, carrying the pain of it into his own life. It didn't excuse my dad's choices, but it gave me a glimpse into why he struggled to be the father I needed. He was fighting battles he didn't know how to win.

Then I wrote about my mum. I wrote about the frustration of watching her drown her emotions in drink, about the pain of feeling like she wasn't there for me when I needed her most. But as I wrote, I started to see her in a new light. I thought about her time in that children's home in Ireland—a place that stripped her of her identity, her family, and her sense of belonging.

I imagined her as a little girl, alone in a cold, loveless institution, learning that vulnerability wasn't safe and kindness was a rare luxury. I thought about the walls she must have built to survive and how those walls kept her from being able to show up fully for me. Maybe she drank because it was the only way she knew how to quiet the ghosts of her past.

By the time I finished, my hand ached, and the page was covered in messy, scrawled words. It wasn't neat or perfect, but that didn't matter. It wasn't for anyone else to read. It was just for me—a chance to give those feelings a place to live outside of me.

I sat for a while, staring at what I'd written. Then, without overthinking it, I folded the paper and held it over the fire. I watched as the edges curled and blackened, the words disappearing into ash.

It wasn't a dramatic, life-changing moment. The weight of my pain didn't vanish in an instant. But it was a start. It was a small act of release, a step toward letting go of the things I'd carried for far too long.

That night in the garden wasn't about fixing everything. It was about creating space for healing to begin. It reminded me that grief doesn't come all at once. It comes in pieces, in quiet moments when we allow ourselves to feel the depth of what was lost and acknowledge the weight we've carried.

For the first time in a long time, I felt like maybe—just maybe—I was ready to take another step forward.

A few years later, I found myself grieving again. This time, it was for my dad. When he passed away in 2019, it brought up a storm of emotions—anger, sadness, regret. The grief wasn't just about losing him; it was about losing the fantasy I'd held onto for so long. The idea that one day he'd get sober and we could do the things other fathers and sons do. I'd always imagined us going on holiday together or sitting down to watch a football match. When he died, that dream died with him.

But here's the thing: the last four years of his life were actually some of the best years we had together. We built a relationship—not perfect, but beautiful in its own way. It had boundaries, which I'll talk about later in this book, but it was real. We connected in ways I never thought possible. And that made losing him even harder, because I wasn't just grieving the man he had been—I was grieving the man he had become, the relationship we had finally found, and the years we would never get to have.

One memory has always stuck with me: every Christmas as a kid, I'd wait for a card or a gift from him. Every year, it never came. That absence became a symbol of the relationship we never had—the father I always dreamed of, the one who might show up one day, take me in his arms, and make everything okay.

After he died, I decided to plant a sweet chestnut tree in my front garden in his honour. I chose the tree carefully—it bears fruit around Christmastime, a quiet reclamation of a season that had always felt heavy for me.

On the first anniversary of his death, I went to the tree. I brought a few personal items that reminded me of him and placed them at its base. Sitting there, I spoke to him— not with rehearsed words, but with raw, unfiltered honesty.

I told him about the anger I'd carried for so long—the times I resented him for not being there, for the chaos he brought into my life, for the pain he caused my mum. I told him about the sadness, the ache of longing for a relationship that didn't come sooner, and the little boy inside me who had waited for him year after year.

And then I let myself feel it all.

As I sat by the tree, the tears came—not in neat, controlled streams, but in waves. They were heavy and relentless, carrying with them the weight of a dream I'd clung to for far too long. These weren't just tears of grief; they were tears of release. I wasn't just mourning his absence—I was mourning the father I had always hoped he could be, the one who would show up one day and save me.

It was as if, for the first time, I truly let go of that fantasy. I let go of the belief that if only I had been better, or different, or more lovable, he would have been the father I needed. Sitting there, under the chestnut tree, I let go of the little boy who waited by the window, hoping this Christmas would be the one.

The tears didn't fix everything, but they lightened something in me. They marked a step forward—not away from the past, but through it. They were a way of honouring what I had lost while reclaiming my life from the weight of it.

Since then, that tree has become a symbol of growth for me. Some years, I visit it and the tears come easily. Other years, I sit quietly, letting its presence remind me of how far I've come. That tree doesn't just stand for my father—it stands for me. For the boy who survived, for the man who learned to let go in a healthy way.

Grieving is one of the hardest things we can do, but it's also one of the most important. It's not about wallowing in pain—it's about honouring what was lost so we can make space for something new. For me, the process began with a campfire and a letter, and later, it deepened with a tree. These moments taught me that grief is not something to avoid—it's something to lean into.

What I learned about grief, though, is that we often don't talk about it. Where I grew up, grieving meant you all went to the pub for the wake, got pissed, and then never spoke about it again. That's just how it was. But for me, that wasn't enough. I had to learn to create something different, something real, something I could touch and feel. Only then could I properly begin to process my grief.

If you're carrying your own pain, I encourage you to find a way to grieve. Write a letter, plant a tree, or create a ritual that feels right for you. Whatever you choose, give yourself the space to feel it all—the anger, the sadness, and even the love. Because in grieving what we've lost, we begin to reclaim what was taken. And in that space, something beautiful can grow.

MOVING TRAUMA THROUGH THE BODY

Trauma isn't just something we carry in our minds—it's also held in our bodies. For years, I misunderstood this, thinking that healing was solely about unpacking the past through dialogue and mental effort. I believed that if I just talked enough, processed enough, and thought hard enough, I could move past the pain. But over time, I came to realize that words alone weren't enough. Trauma embeds itself not just in our minds but physically—within our muscles, our posture, and even our breath.

Back in 2009, eighteen months into sobriety, I impulsively signed up for the London Marathon. It felt like a ridiculous idea. After years of alcohol and drug abuse, compounded by the time I'd spent locked away in a tiny cell for 23 hours a day, I was certain my body wasn't capable of achieving something so demanding. But there was something about the challenge that called to me—a chance to prove to myself that I could do more than just survive.

I started training along the towpath from Isleworth to Richmond, gradually extending my runs into Richmond Park. At first, every step was a struggle. My body ached, protesting in ways I'd never experienced before. I doubted myself constantly, wondering if I'd made a huge mistake. But as the miles added up, something began to shift. Running became more than just physical exercise—it became a form of meditation. The open spaces of Richmond Park, the sound of my breath, and the steady rhythm of my feet on the path began to feel like freedom. With every step, I felt like I was reclaiming parts of myself I thought were lost.

Science supports the profound impact of exercise on mental health. Studies, including one from *JAMA Psychiatry*, show that regular exercise can combat symptoms of PTSD and depression as effectively as medication. Just 30 minutes of moderate exercise, five times a week, can enhance mood and emotional well-being. For someone like me, who had lived for years in chaos, this was transformative.

Exercise also combats high cortisol levels, the stress hormone that keeps us locked in fight-or-flight mode. For those healing from trauma, this is a constant state of being. According to a review in *Frontiers in Psychology*, physical activity helps regulate our stress responses, fostering calm and grounding. Additionally, exercise stimulates endorphins—the body's natural mood lifters—enhancing feelings of happiness and well-being after just 20 minutes of activity.

Training for the marathon taught me something I never expected: healing isn't just about sitting still; it's about movement. It's about letting your body release what it's been holding for far too long.

But running wasn't the only thing that helped me heal. Martial arts, particularly Brazilian jiu-jitsu, became a critical part of my recovery. For someone like me, whose life had been shaped by violent, uncontrolled fights—fights driven by rage and the need to win at all costs—stepping into a structured space of combat seemed almost counter-intuitive. Who would have guessed that entering a combat sport and learning a new way of doing things could be so healing?

Jiu-jitsu taught me that not every fight has to be a battle for survival. It introduced me to the concept of control, of strategy, of using technique instead of brute force. For the first time, I began to see other men not as threats, but as training partners—people who wanted to help me improve, who pushed me to become better.

This shift was monumental for me. The same hands that once fought in anger were now used to shake hands before and after every match. The same mind that once sought to destroy was now learning to build trust and camaraderie. It was more than just physical training—it was a re-education of the way I saw myself and others.

Research supports the profound impact of martial arts on mental health. An article in the *Journal of Bodywork and*

Movement Therapies suggests that martial arts training can be an effective intervention for improving mental health outcomes. It helps develop psychological resilience, improves physical coordination, and fosters a sense of belonging within a supportive community.

If you're carrying something heavy, I encourage you to move. It doesn't have to be a marathon or a martial arts class. It can start small—a walk, a morning stretch, or a few deep breaths. Trauma doesn't just live in your mind; it's held in your body. And your body doesn't just harbour trauma—it also possesses a profound capacity for releasing it.

THE SWEAT LODGE

For those who've never experienced a sweat lodge, it's hard to put into words exactly what it is. At its core, it's a sacred ceremony, rooted in Indigenous traditions, especially among Native American and First Nations peoples. The lodge itself is a low, dome-shaped structure made of natural materials like willow branches, covered tightly with blankets or tarps to seal in the heat. Inside, stones are heated to a glowing red in a fire and brought into the lodge, where water is poured over them to create steam.

But a sweat lodge is so much more than just a structure or a process—it's a place of purification, prayer, and connection. It represents the womb of Mother Earth, a space where you can release what no longer serves you and reconnect with the sacred.

I first stepped into a sweat lodge in 2014, and I can honestly say it changed the course of my life. At the time,

I'd been sober for a few years and was already searching for deeper meaning. Sobriety had brought clarity, but it had also opened the door to questions I didn't have answers to—questions about spirituality, about how to pray, and about where I fit in the bigger picture of life.

When I first stepped into a sweat lodge, I was sceptical, fearful, and even a little judgmental. Though I'd always been intrigued by Native American spirituality—thanks in part to films like *Dances with Wolves*—I didn't fully understand its depth or significance. That all changed during my first sweat lodge ceremony in Scotland. It was snowing, and the group was all men.

Crawling into the lodge on my hands and knees, I felt the weight of the experience immediately. The darkness wasn't just the absence of light—it was a space that stripped everything away, forcing me to confront myself. As the heat intensified and the chanting began, I felt old tensions and emotions rise to the surface—anger, pain, things I'd buried for years.

There were moments when I wanted to escape, to run from the intensity. It reminded me of the ways I'd numbed myself in the past, but this time, I stayed. And in that decision, something broke open inside me. A primal roar erupted from deep within, followed by tears—not of sadness, but of release.

The heat, the songs, the presence of the other men—it was profoundly healing. The lodge wasn't just a place of discomfort; it was a place of connection, transformation, and truth. That first experience taught me to lean into the discomfort, to let go, and to honour the process of healing. It was the beginning of a deeper understanding of myself and the sacredness of this journey.

That first sweat lodge was just the beginning for me. Over the years, as I continued to follow this path, I was invited to reservations across the United States to deepen my understanding of these sacred ways. I learned from elders, from medicine men and women who had spent their lives protecting these traditions.

Eventually, after almost a decade of walking this path, I earned the honour of having my own lodge in the UK—a gift granted by a Lakota holy man, a *Wicasa Wakan*. This wasn't something given lightly. To earn this right, I had to complete *Hanblechyia,* a vision quest, which involved spending four days and three nights inside a lodge with no food or water, just my prayers and the darkness.

When I say prayers, you might imagine something religious—reciting lines in a church or temple, sitting in neat rows wearing your Sunday best. But this couldn't be further from what I mean.

In Native American tradition, prayers are something entirely different. They are primal, raw, and deeply connected to the Earth and all living things. We often say *Aho Mitakuye Oyasin*, which translates to "We are all related." When we pray, it's not about speaking to a distant god in the sky—it's about speaking with our relations and loved ones, past and present. It's about connecting with Mother Nature, the stars, the great unknown, or what we call the Great Spirit.

Prayers in this sense are deeply personal. They're not about asking for things or following a rehearsed set of lines. They're about speaking from your heart—raw, unfiltered, and honest. It's a dialogue with life itself, with the unseen forces that have shaped us and the natural world that holds us.

Those four days were some of the most challenging and transformative of my life. Sitting with nothing but my thoughts and prayers, I connected with my ancestors in ways I hadn't thought possible. The experience showed me things I hadn't been ready to see before, and by the end of the fourth day, I didn't want to leave.

The monthly practice of sitting in a sweat lodge has profoundly shaped my understanding of healing. It's taught me that healing isn't just about letting go of pain—it's about transforming it into something sacred and meaningful. The heat, the darkness, and the songs create a space where you can fully feel, release tension, and reconnect with something greater than yourself.

On a physical level, the heat helps detoxify your body, flushing out impurities and boosting circulation, while the steam can improve respiratory function. The process also stimulates the release of endorphins, reducing stress and leaving you with a deep sense of calm and balance.

Emotionally, the lodge provides a safe and supportive environment to process buried emotions, fostering clarity and a sense of renewal. Spiritually, it reconnects you with nature, your ancestors, and your inner self, grounding you in the present moment.

Even now, whether I'm leading a lodge or sitting in one, I'm reminded of its power. It cuts through the noise of life and brings you back to what truly matters. For me, the sweat lodge has been life-changing. And for anyone willing to step into that sacred space, I believe it holds the power to change yours too.

A WORD OF CAUTION: PRACTICING SAFELY

Sweat lodges are deeply healing but must be approached with care and respect. When led by unqualified individuals, they can become dangerous, and sadly, lives have been lost because of poor practice.

Traditionally, only those granted the proper rites by a medicine man or elder are qualified to lead a lodge. This ensures the ceremony is conducted safely and honours its sacred traditions.

If you're considering participating, ensure the leader has been properly trained and is transparent about their experience. Respect the ceremony, listen to your body, and know it's okay to step out if the heat becomes overwhelming.

Done right, the sweat lodge is transformative. But it requires proper leadership and reverence to ensure everyone's safety and the integrity of the tradition.

THERAPY

Therapy has been a cornerstone of my healing journey, and I wouldn't be the man I am today without it. But let me be honest—the path to embracing therapy wasn't smooth.

My first encounter with therapy was in prison after my suicide attempt. I was a young man, raw, broken, and completely lost. Therapy wasn't something I chose; it was forced upon me. I was made to sit across from a therapist—a man I knew nothing about, a stranger who felt like he was there just to tick a box. I was given three sessions, barely enough time to say what was on my mind, let alone build trust or safety. And then it was over.

It's no surprise that my opinion of therapy and therapists was negative after that experience. How could I believe in the process when it felt so transactional, so surface-level? I was drowning, and it felt like someone had tossed me a thimble instead of a life raft.

It wasn't until years later, after I got sober, that therapy became something I chose—and something that became a lifeline. Sobriety gave me clarity, and with clarity came a deep desire to heal. For the first time, I started to see my life and patterns for what they really were.

With the help of my AA sponsor, Sean, I found safety—the first vital step. Sean wasn't just a sponsor; he was the first person who held space for me without judgment. He allowed me to feel seen in a way I hadn't experienced before. That safety gave me the foundation to move into the next stage of healing: awareness. I began to understand the issues I carried, the layers of pain I'd buried for so long.

From there, therapy became a place where honesty could take root, where I could begin to unpack my trauma with someone who had the expertise to challenge my way of thinking. It became a sounding board, a space where I could explore the parts of myself I'd been too scared to face.

And for someone like me—someone whose parents weren't the most supportive for most of my life—that has been invaluable. Therapy has been like having someone in my corner, someone who's there solely to help me navigate the mess of life, even if I've had to pay for it. That expertise has been worth every penny.

Looking back, I can see how therapy helped me move through the stages of healing that this book has covered—finding safety, building awareness, and stepping into honesty. It's where I put all of those pieces into practice. Therapy gave me the space to unpack the layers of my trauma, navigate relationships, and process the intense emotions that surfaced as I walked this path.

Over the years, I've learned to tailor my approach to therapy based on what I needed at the time. For issues related to women or my mum, I worked with female therapists who could help me understand those dynamics. For deeper wounds tied to my dad or masculinity, I worked with male therapists. Eventually, I settled with a male therapist I've been with for seven years now—a relationship that has been a steady anchor in my life.

But therapy isn't always straightforward. It requires effort, patience, and the willingness to be honest with yourself. And let's be real—therapy isn't a magic fix, nor is it always the right fit for everyone at every stage. Research shows that men, in particular, face unique challenges when it comes to engaging with therapy. Many men who take their own lives were in therapy at the time, which is a sobering reminder that therapy alone isn't enough. It's a tool—a powerful one—but it needs to be paired with the right support, the right connection, and a commitment to doing the work.

For me, that work only became possible after sobriety. Getting sober wasn't just about putting down the drink; it was about facing everything I'd used alcohol to numb. Therapy helped me take that raw, unfiltered clarity and turn it into a deeper understanding of myself. Together, sobriety and therapy gave me the tools to step out of survival mode and into a place of growth and purpose.

If you're considering therapy, know that it's a process. Finding the right therapist can take time, and it's okay if it doesn't click right away. What matters is creating a space where you feel safe enough to start being honest—with your therapist, and most importantly, with yourself. Therapy isn't about fixing you because you're broken—it's about uncovering the truth of who you are and finding ways to live in alignment with that truth.

For people like me, who didn't grow up with supportive parents or stable foundations, having someone in your corner—even if you have to pay for it—can be life-changing. Therapy isn't always easy, but it's one of the best investments I've ever made.

THE POWER OF COACHING, SPONSORSHIP, AND MENTORSHIP

Healing from trauma, transforming your life, and stepping into your potential is not a journey you can—or should—take alone. Along the way, I've learned that having mentors, coaches, and sponsors has been invaluable. These relationships have shaped every aspect of my life, from getting sober to building my business, learning how to help others, and even running sweat lodges safely and with integrity.

Some of the most important lessons I've learned weren't from books or courses, but from people who had walked the path before me. These mentors shared their wisdom, their experiences, and their time. Some helped me voluntarily, out of their own desire to give back. Others I sought out and paid for their expertise. One truth has become clear to me: if I want to achieve something, and I don't know how to do it, I just need to find someone who has—and ask them to help me.

In my journey to sobriety, my AA sponsor was one of the first people who taught me the power of having someone in your corner. He had been where I was, and he knew the steps I needed to take to move forward. His guidance wasn't just about giving advice—it was about listening, holding me accountable, and reminding me that I wasn't alone.

As I began to grow and heal, I sought out other mentors and coaches to guide me in new areas of life. When I started my business, I recruited a coach to help me navigate the challenges of leadership and entrepreneurship. When

I was called forward to lead sweat lodges, I worked with respected elders to ensure I was equipped to do it safely and respectfully. Each of these relationships added to my growth in ways I couldn't have managed on my own.

The truth is, we need more mentors in the world. We need people who are willing to share their gifts, their knowledge, and their time. For young men, especially those who don't have fathers in their lives, mentorship can be life-changing. Studies have shown that boys without a father figure are at a higher risk of poor educational outcomes, substance abuse, and involvement in crime. But with the guidance of a mentor, those risks can be significantly reduced.

Research in sports provides a powerful example of the impact of mentorship. Athletes with strong coaches and mentors not only perform better but also develop resilience, discipline, and confidence that extend beyond the playing field. A 2020 study by the Journal of Adolescent Health found that mentoring relationships reduced depressive symptoms and increased self-esteem in young people, particularly those facing adversity.

For me, mentors and coaches have been more than just teachers—they've been mirrors, reflecting back the potential I couldn't always see in myself. They've reminded me of what's possible when you're willing to learn, to listen, and to do the work.

If you're on this journey of healing or transformation, I encourage you to seek out mentors, coaches, or sponsors. Look for people who have walked the road you want to travel and ask them for guidance. Sometimes that guidance will come as a gift, freely given. Other times, you'll need to invest in yourself and pay for their expertise. Either way, it's worth it.

And if you're in a place where you have gifts to share, consider becoming a mentor yourself. The world needs more people who are willing to give back, to hold out a hand, and to help someone else find their way. Because when we share what we've learned, we're not just helping others—we're building a legacy of connection, wisdom, and transformation that can ripple out far beyond our own lives.

THE POWER OF BREATHWORK: RELEASING TRAUMA THROUGH THE BODY

Back in 2012, I had my first experience with breathwork. At the time, it wasn't as widely known as it is today, and to be honest, I wasn't sure what to expect. Someone in the recovery community had introduced me to it, describing it as a way to access and release deeply buried emotions. I was curious but sceptical. After years of therapy, AA meetings, and personal reflection, I still felt like there was something stuck inside me—something no amount of talking had been able to reach.

The session began simply enough. The facilitator asked me to lie down, close my eyes, and focus on my breath. They guided me into a rhythm—deep inhale, strong exhale, repeated over and over again. At first, it felt awkward, even ridiculous. My mind raced with thoughts like, *What am I doing here? Can this really help me?*

But as I stayed with the breath, something incredible began to happen.

My body started to shake. My chest tightened, as though it was bracing itself for something big. Then, like a dam breaking, emotions I hadn't even realized I'd been holding onto came rushing to the surface. It was like I was revisiting the scene of the crime—reliving the traumas of my childhood, not just in my mind but in my body.

I screamed. A deep, guttural roar erupted from somewhere I didn't even know existed. It wasn't calculated or planned—it was primal, raw, and completely uncontrollable. I shouted. I sobbed. Tears streamed down my face, mixing with snot, as wave after wave of grief and anger poured out of me.

And then, in the middle of it all, I thought of her. Sacha, my partner of just over a year at the time, the woman who would one day become my wife. I thought of all the trauma I had carried inside me, the things she didn't even know about because I had been too scared to tell her. I feared that if she knew the truth, if she saw the weight I carried, she might reject me. But in that moment, it all came to the surface—the pain, the fear, the longing to be seen, and, most importantly, the desire to be better.

Not just for me, but for her. For us. For the life we wanted to create together.

The memories weren't just thoughts—they were physical. I felt them in my chest, in my stomach, in the tension that had been living in my body for decades. I cried for the boy I was, for the things I had endured, for the pain I had buried so deeply I'd almost forgotten it was there.

It wasn't pretty. It wasn't neat. It was messy, wild, overwhelming—and absolutely necessary.

On the other side of it, something remarkable happened.

I found peace.

It felt like the trauma that had been trapped inside me for so long had finally found a way out. My body felt lighter, freer. For the first time in as long as I could remember, I could truly breathe. And with that release came clarity—a vision of the life I wanted to build, a life rooted in love, honesty, and connection.

That first breathwork journey was profound. It wasn't just healing—it was transformative. It gave me access to parts of myself I hadn't been able to reach through words or reflection alone. It showed me that trauma isn't just something we carry in our minds—it lives in our bodies. And to truly heal, we have to release it from where it's been hiding.

This experience was a turning point for me. I was so moved by the power of breathwork that I began training in it, learning everything I could about its ability to help regulate the nervous system and release trauma. Today, I use a variety of breathwork methods in my work, tailoring them to meet people where they are in their healing journey.

Breathwork isn't about looking good or keeping it together. It's about letting go, about giving yourself permission to feel everything that's been buried for too long. It's not always easy, but the freedom on the other side is worth every moment of discomfort.

If you've been carrying something heavy, if you've felt like words alone haven't been enough, I invite you to explore the power of your breath. It's more than a tool—it's a lifeline to the parts of yourself that are ready to heal.

BREATHWORK AND TRAUMA: THE SCIENCE

Breathwork isn't just a powerful personal experience—it's also supported by research. Studies have shown that intentional breathing practices can significantly impact the way we process trauma and regulate our nervous system.

One study published in the *Journal of Traumatic Stress* found that individuals who engaged in controlled breathing exercises experienced reduced symptoms of PTSD, such as hyperarousal and intrusive thoughts. Another study from *Frontiers in Psychology* highlighted that breath-focused practices like coherent breathing directly impact the vagus nerve, which plays a critical role in calming the body and reducing the fight-or-flight response associated with trauma.

Breathwork has also been shown to increase heart rate variability (HRV), a key marker of how well the body can regulate stress. Higher HRV is associated with better emotional resilience and the ability to recover from traumatic experiences.

For those who've experienced trauma, the body often holds onto the pain long after the event has passed. Trauma gets stored in the muscles, tissues, and nervous system, creating a constant state of tension or numbness. Breathwork offers a way to release that tension, not through the mind, but through the body itself.

EP - EMOTIONAL PROCESSING

Of all the tools I've used to process everything I went through, emotional processing has been the most transformative. It's a method I first encountered at an event run by Clearmind International, led by Duane and Catherine O'Kane. Their approach opened my eyes to the possibility of true healing—healing that doesn't just skim the surface but dives deep into the core of our pain.

In other spaces, this work is called different things. Some refer to it as carpet work, shadow work, or guts work. I call it emotional processing, but my way of doing it is a bit different from others. It's a method I've developed over the years, drawing on everything I've learned from the training I've undertaken since 2007. It mirrors the same structure as the chapters in this book.

Let me explain what emotional processing looks like for someone who's never encountered it before. At its core, this practice invites a participant to step into the middle of a supportive circle of people. This space is created with the intention of safety, respect, and care. The person in the centre is guided to share something they're struggling with—whether it's a present challenge or unresolved pain from the past.

The facilitator's job is to create a process that allows the participant to explore and send healing to that part of their life. It might involve recreating the dynamics of a past event or helping the participant connect with a younger version of themselves. The aim is to bring insight and compassion to the pain, allowing the person to release it, evolve the issue, and move forward with a new mindset.

My first experience stepping into the circle was life-changing. I was guided to revisit the difficulties of my childhood, growing up in a home where sexual abuse had occurred. My home felt like a war zone—unsafe, chaotic, and filled with fear.

And in the middle of all that emotion, in the heartache of witnessing his pain and the pain of my parents, I realized what needed to change. That little boy didn't need fixing—he needed to feel heard, to feel held, to know he was enough.

In that moment, I decided to offer that to him, my younger self. It seems strange writing this now, but in that moment, it felt so real. If the facilitator is skilled enough—and in this case, they were—you find yourself fully invested in the process.

I had chosen John, a soft-spoken Irishman from Cork, to play my younger self. There was something about him, a childlike innocence in his eyes, that made him feel right for this role. He was around my age, but in that moment, he became the little boy I once was.

I got down on my knees and looked into John's eyes. The words came from somewhere deep inside me. "It's not your fault," I said, my voice trembling. "None of it was your fault. You're not bad. You're not like your father. I'm sorry."

After that, I leaned in and hugged him. It wasn't just a gesture—it was everything I had never been able to give myself. And as I held him, we both cried. Not polite, quiet tears, but the kind that come from somewhere raw and unspoken.

It had landed somewhere deep for John too. I could feel it in the way his body shook as we embraced. Those words had stirred something in him as well. In that moment, it wasn't just about me—it was about the shared humanity of our pain, the unspoken burdens we carry, and the healing that can happen when we truly connect.

That process was one of the most pivotal moments of my journey. I cried for that little boy, for the pain he endured, for the love he didn't receive. And in doing so, I began to release some of the weight I'd been carrying for years.

This work also gave me clarity about who I wanted to become. At this stage in my life, I was deeply committed to being a better partner to Sacha and a better father to my children. These moments of emotional processing weren't just about healing my past—they were about shaping my future. They were about breaking the cycle, so I could show up fully for the people I love most.

In 2014, I encountered this kind of work again in a different form—shadow work with the Mankind Project.

Shadow work involves looking at the parts of ourselves we've hidden or denied, often because they feel too painful or shameful to face. In this process, I came to a startling realization: I had hidden and denied the part of myself that was soft and gentle.

I'd buried it so deeply that it felt easier to punch someone in the face for talking disrespectfully to me than it did to simply say, "Please don't talk to me like that." That was the man I was back then—angry, quick to lose my temper, and always ready to fight. It was the man I had to be to survive in the world I grew up in. But through this work, I saw that part of me clearly for the first time, and I began to understand how much I needed to welcome it back into my life.

Ironically, this realization came at the perfect time— 2014 was the year my daughter Sienna was born. My daughters have had a beautiful way of softening me, of showing me that being gentle and kind is a strength, not a weakness. I often think that's why I've been blessed with three daughters—they've taught me how to embrace that softer side of myself.

That shadow work allowed me to welcome the gentleness back into my life and to bring it with me as I moved forward. It wasn't about leaving the strength and resilience behind—it was about finding balance, allowing both parts of me to exist together. And for that, I'll always be grateful.

Both experiences reinforced a powerful truth: we carry the pain of our past in our bodies, our subconscious, and the choices we make. But we don't have to carry it forever.

Emotional processing offers a way to confront that pain directly, to understand it, and to release it.

I've stepped into the middle of that circle to do this kind of work more than fifty times now, and I'll continue to do my own personal work. I believe it's part of our journey to heal our traumas—not just for ourselves, but for those who come after us.

This kind of work, in my experience, can achieve what might take years of therapy in just one powerful session. It's not easy, but it's transformative. It allows you to address the deepest wounds with compassion and understanding, to send healing to the parts of you that need it most, and to move forward with a new perspective on life.

THE IMPORTANCE OF EXPERIENCE AND INTEGRITY

In recent years, the conversation around healing and self-development has expanded dramatically. Practices like shadow work, emotional processing, trauma healing, breathwork, and cold water therapy have moved from the fringes into the mainstream. Now, it seems everyone might be a breathwork coach, transformational coach, or life coach. This shift is largely driven by our current mental health crisis, and as we've often seen in the West, it doesn't take long for a market to emerge around such a crisis.

On one hand, this development is positive—it's opening up discussions about mental health and encouraging people to seek help. However, there are significant risks involved. As these practices become more popular, there's a real danger they might lose their essence, becoming commodified—packaged, branded, and sold as the next big trend.

Today, celebrities, influencers, and podcasters are launching retreats and events under the wellness banner, promoting the idea that healing is something you can purchase and achieve in a single session. But genuine healing isn't a product. It isn't something that can be neatly packaged, priced, and sold to those who can afford it.

If we allow this field to become overly commercialized and transactional, we risk making these vital services accessible only to the affluent, pushing those in greatest need even further away. Healing spaces shouldn't be exclusive to those who can pay—their doors should be open to everyone, regardless of financial standing.

That's why protecting the integrity of the healing and self-development field is so crucial. It's not only about having the right people facilitate these practices but ensuring they're not just in it for financial gain. Healing is a sacred, often messy journey that demands deep personal commitment. It's not a trend, a brand, or a quick fix.

When I first engaged with this work in 2007, I wasn't chasing a fad. I entered those spaces broken, seeking genuine transformation, not a superficial experience. The environments I embraced promoted a message of ongoing commitment, not overnight solutions. Healing is a lifestyle, demanding continual dedication.

Taking on the role of facilitating this work is a profound responsibility. Guiding someone through their healing process is akin to holding their soul in your hands—a role that should never be taken lightly. It demands integrity, empathy, and a relentless dedication to one's own healing journey.

Unfortunately, it's all too common to see individuals lead these spaces without having engaged deeply with their own healing. Some might even use leadership as a diversion from facing their personal pain, focusing outward to avoid looking inward. This approach can be detrimental, sometimes disastrously so. Similar to the issues seen with poorly facilitated sweat lodges, where lives have been tragically lost, inadequate leadership in healing spaces can lead people into deep psychological territories they're not prepared for. Tragically, it's not uncommon for individuals to leave such events feeling more lost, some to the extent of taking their own lives. This is the uncomfortable truth I feel compelled to speak on—not because I wish to position myself as the ultimate authority but because recognizing these dangers is crucial.

I didn't start to facilitate emotional processing workshops until I was eleven years deep into my own healing journey, equipped with extensive training and personal experience. Even now, I approach this work with the utmost respect and caution.

For anyone considering entering these healing spaces, either as a participant or a facilitator, please proceed with discernment. Ask about the facilitator's training, their experience, and ongoing personal work. Question whether their services are accessible to those who can't afford to pay.

Healing is a profound, ongoing process that requires wisdom and deep respect.

This work is too crucial to be led by the unprepared, and it's too important to be exclusive to the wealthy. We have a duty to ensure that healing remains accessible and is approached with the seriousness it warrants. Anything less does a disservice to the healing journey of all involved.

CONNECTION IS THE MEDICINE

Processing pain isn't something we're meant to do alone. Johann Hari captures this essence perfectly when he says, "The opposite of addiction is not sobriety; it's connection." This perspective is pivotal in understanding healing. To truly process our pain, we need the support of others—people who can hold space for us, understand us, and remind us that we are not alone in our struggles. Through the power of connection, we find the communal support, strength, and perspective essential for profound healing.

At the events I run, we live by a simple slogan: "*Connection is the Medicine*". Over and over, I've seen how true this is. Whether it's in a community, a brotherhood, or a fellowship, the power of human connection is the foundation of healing. Trauma isolates us, convincing us that we're on our own. But connection brings us back to life. It reminds us that healing isn't a solitary journey—it's one we walk alongside others.

Research supports this truth. Peer support groups, where people with shared experiences come together to help one another, have been shown to significantly improve mental health outcomes. A 2017 study published in The Journal of Community Psychology found that peer support reduced feelings of isolation, increased emotional resilience, and led to improved coping strategies in individuals facing trauma. This is especially true for men, who often struggle to seek help due to societal expectations around vulnerability. Being part of a group where others say, "Me too," can be life-changing.

In my own journey, having a safe space to process my pain made all the difference. I'll never forget attending a meeting with the Mankind Project in Fulham back in 2015. At the time, my life felt overwhelming. Oakhill was going through some difficulties, things at home were tough, and Sienna had been born the year before. We needed a bigger place, and I carried the weight of it all—sometimes silently, not wanting to burden Sacha with it. I felt like the pressure was relentless, and I found myself in this circle of men, ready to let it all out.

At these gatherings, we would set aside time for any man who wanted to take some space in the middle of the circle. That night, I stepped in. The facilitator asked me, "What do you want to have happen here?" I said, "I just want to be heard and seen."

The men came closer, forming a tighter circle around me. The facilitator asked me to close my eyes and let them in. I started speaking, my voice heavy with emotion. "I find this so hard—trying to create a life for my family. It's so hard carrying this all on my own. I feel so alone at times. I wish I had a father to guide and support me. I feel like I'm not strong enough to do all of this. Sometimes I just want to quit…"

With that final statement, I let out a deep breath. It was like I'd been holding it in for years, and as I exhaled, I felt a huge release of tension. The facilitator noticed and said, "Do that again, Michael. Let out another deep breath." So I did, and this time, I felt the weight of it all lift off me. I fell to my knees and cried.

The men around me didn't offer words of encouragement or magic solutions. They didn't try to fix me. They just stood there, in silence, stepping closer to place a hand on me. It wasn't about solving anything—it was about connection. It was about brotherhood.

That's what connection looks like. Healing doesn't happen in isolation—it happens in moments like this. When one person speaks their truth and others stand with them, not to fix or judge, but simply to hold space.

If you're on this journey, remember this: you don't have to do it alone. Whether it's a friend, a peer support group, or even just one person who understands, reach out. Let someone walk this road with you. Connection really is the medicine. And in that connection, you might find the strength and safety you need to take the next step.

PLANT MEDICINE

In this section, we explore a topic that might be met with scepticism by many, especially within the medical community: plant medicine. Though my personal experience with this form of therapy is minimal, I feel it's important to share the profound impact it has had on the lives of two men I know well. Their transformations were so significant that to omit their stories from our discussion on trauma healing would not only be unfair but also a disservice to those searching for hope.

The first story is about David, a man whose life I've been connected to through my volunteer work in prisons. David's backstory is marked by hardship—growing up without a father, surviving sexual abuse, and being exploited by local gangs due to his size. His role as an enforcer for drug dealers landed him in prison multiple times. Upon his last release in 2019, he attended one of our CIP events. I saw a man on the brink, someone who could easily slip back into his old life. During this time, he mentioned an upcoming meeting with a South American shaman to try Ayahuasca, a powerful plant-based medicine. We lost touch for a few months, and when we finally reconnected, I met a completely transformed David. He was calm, centred, and spoke of spirituality and purpose in ways I had never heard from him before. His journey since then has been remarkable—he has stayed out of prison and is now helping others heal through the same means that dramatically altered his course.

Then there's Rob, a friend from Boston and a military veteran who served in Iraq. When I first met him, Rob was a shadow of the man he once was. The toll of his service was visible in his weary eyes and withdrawn demeanour. Years later, on a return trip to Boston, a vibrant and lively man greeted me at the airport. It was Rob, but not the Rob I remembered. He explained that he had found an organization called Veterans Exploring Treatment Solutions, which led him to South America to engage with plant medicine. The impact on his PTSD was transformative.

I understand that discussing plant medicine might raise eyebrows or even draw criticism from some medical professionals. However, witnessing the undeniable transformations of David and Rob compels me to include their experiences here. The emerging research on plant medicines like Ayahuasca offers promising results, notably in the treatment of PTSD and other severe trauma-related disorders. Studies, including those published in reputable journals such as the *Journal of Psychopharmacology*, have documented significant and lasting reductions in symptoms of depression and anxiety following Ayahuasca therapy.

By sharing these stories and supporting data, I'm not dismissing traditional treatments but rather highlighting an additional option that might be the key for those who have yet to find relief. It's about providing every possible tool for healing, especially for those who feel they have exhausted all other avenues. If this chapter offers new avenues for healing or simply sparks a deeper inquiry into alternative therapies, then it will have served its purpose. It's about looking out for each other, exploring all our options, and supporting one another on our journeys to healing and wholeness.

THE CURRENT STATE OF AFFAIRS

In this chapter, we've explored many of the methods that have shaped my healing journey—sweat lodges, breathwork, emotional processing, therapy, connection with community, coaching, mentorship, grieving, moving pain through the body, exercise, plant medicine and martial arts. Each of these didn't just offer temporary relief; they helped me uncover the roots of my pain, where real transformation happens.

The reality, though, is that while these methods exist in the UK, they remain out of reach for many. Therapy, for instance, is widely recognized as a tool for healing, but long NHS waiting lists make it inaccessible for those who can't afford private care. Over 1.2 million people are waiting for mental health support, with delays of eighteen weeks or longer. When you're struggling, that kind of wait can feel unbearable.

Other methods—sweat lodges, emotional processing, breathwork, plant medicine, and martial arts—are available, but there are barriers to accessing them. Many require financial resources, which puts them out of reach for those on low incomes. Even widely available practices like exercise and martial arts often don't highlight their potential as tools for trauma recovery, leaving many unaware of how they can help.

I know this struggle firsthand. In the early years of my healing journey, I saved every spare penny to attend seminars, events, and workshops. I knew I needed these tools to change my life, but the financial burden was enormous. And it's hard not to wonder—what if these resources had been more accessible? What if they were offered in schools, prisons, or community centres? My journey may not have taken as long if these tools had been available to people like me, who were struggling financially but desperate for change.

The lack of accessibility isn't just about money—it's about systemic priorities. Many of these practices challenge conventional systems of care. They require facilitators with integrity and lived experience, spaces that prioritize safety, and approaches that go beyond surface-level solutions. These demands make them harder to implement within traditional structures like prisons, schools, and rehabs.

Prisons, for example, often focus on punishment rather than rehabilitation. A 2021 report from the Prison Reform Trust highlighted how little room there is for therapeutic approaches that address the root causes of criminal behaviour, like unresolved trauma. Similarly, schools prioritize behaviour management over emotional healing, and gyms and martial arts spaces rarely highlight their potential for mental health recovery.

This gap in accessibility isn't just about systems—it's about fairness. Healing should not be reserved for those who can afford it. The methods I've written about in this chapter—methods that have helped me transform my life—should be available to everyone, regardless of income or background.

At my charity and in the organizations I work with, we aim to do things differently. We offer free bursary places to anyone who cannot afford to pay. In fact, 99% of the work we do is funded by voluntary donations from people who believe in our mission. It's our way of ensuring that healing isn't reserved for the privileged but is accessible to anyone who truly needs it.

This isn't just a message for retreat leaders or wellness practitioners—it's a message for governments, schools, and the people running our prisons and rehabs. Research shows that community-based, trauma-informed approaches significantly reduce reoffending rates and improve mental health outcomes. A 2020 study from the *International Journal of Offender Therapy and Comparative Criminology* found that peer support and emotional processing programs in prisons reduced reoffending rates by up to 30%. Similarly, exercise and martial arts have been shown to reduce symptoms of anxiety and PTSD, helping people regulate their nervous systems and rebuild trust in themselves and others.

We can bring about real change—not by anger or division, but by speaking our truth, supporting organizations doing meaningful work, and ensuring these life-changing methods are accessible to everyone. Healing should be a human right, not a privilege for the few. Together, we can make that a reality.

THE COURAGE TO HEAL

Processing pain is not an easy journey. It's messy, uncomfortable, and at times, it feels overwhelming. But it's also profoundly transformative. The work I've shared in this chapter—sweat lodges, breathwork, emotional processing, therapy, connection, grieving, moving pain through the body, and so much more—has been my lifeline. These weren't just tools; they were the keys that unlocked the door to my freedom.

You might wonder why I've gone through all of this. If you've seen photos of my wife and daughters, there's your answer. I do it for them. For Sacha, for my girls, for the life we're building together. I do it to break the cycle of anger, chaos, and pain that I was raised in, so my children don't have to carry those burdens.

But it's bigger than just my family. When we commit to our journey, we're not just changing our own lives—we're raising the consciousness of humanity. Every step we take toward wholeness is a step toward breaking generational cycles, healing our communities, and creating a better world. Not through grand gestures, but through the quiet, powerful act of showing up—for ourselves and for those we love.

This work isn't about erasing the past. It's about transforming it into something meaningful. It's about reclaiming your power, breaking the chains that have held you back, and creating a life that feels lighter, freer, and filled with purpose. That's the life I live today—a life I couldn't have imagined for myself years ago. By all accounts, I shouldn't be here. I was angry, violent, an addict, and a convicted armed robber. That man feels unrecognizable to me now.

The transformation I've experienced didn't happen by chance—it happened because of the work I've shared in this chapter. And it's work you can do too. You don't have to wait for the perfect moment or circumstances. Start where you are.

Take a step. It doesn't have to be a big one—maybe it's therapy, breathwork, writing a letter, joining a community, or simply moving your body. Whatever resonates, trust it. Every small, brave step takes you closer to the peace and wholeness you deserve.

This work isn't just about you—it's about the people you love. I do this for Sacha, for my girls, and for the world I want them to grow up in. They're my "why," the reason I keep going when the road feels too hard.

Look around and find your "why" too. It could be your family, your friends, your dreams—or it could simply be *you*. You are worth doing this for.

As we move into the next chapter—Connection—reflect on what resonated with you here. Think about what processing pain has taught you. This isn't about following my path or anyone else's. It's about finding your own way, just as I found mine.

———

CHAPTER 5

CONNECTION

"Connection is the antidote to isolation. It's the bridge that leads us back to ourselves, our loved ones, and the world around us."

THE BEAUTIFUL BURDEN

Imagine walking through a dense, prickly hedge backwards—emerging on the other side feeling raw, exposed, and disorientated. That's what this journey feels like at first when your on the other side of doing the work we spoke about in chapter four. But there's more to this journey. The real, profound work begins once you step out of that hedge: reconnecting with yourself, with those around you who were touched by your pain, and with the world that felt so distant.

When you've walked through the shadow of your own suffering and come out stronger, you're no longer the person you were. You carry within you a profound lived experience, a depth most people might never know. You've stared down your darkest moments and have been reforged by them into someone more aware, more compassionate, and infinitely stronger.

This transformation, while deeply personal, isn't just for you. It bestows upon you a beautiful yet heavy responsibility. Recovering from difficult life experiences grant us a moral obligation, a sacred task to extend a hand to those still in the throes of their battles. It's as if you've been given a torch; not just to light your path, but to illuminate the way for others. This, I call the beautiful burden. It's a challenging role, but richly rewarding.

The act of reconnecting after trauma is not merely about mending what was broken. It's about finding meaning in the pain you've endured and leveraging that pain to contribute to the world in ways you might never have imagined. Through reconnecting, we discover purpose, we foster belonging, and we find love.

And there's something miraculous that happens when you've done this inner work. Don't be surprised if people are drawn to you, like moths to a flame. You might find strangers opening up to you about their pain, sharing their stories without even knowing why. This is a sign, a clear signal that the work you're doing is powerful and effective. It's a reminder to keep pushing forward, to keep shining your light. The world is in desperate need of more hope, more light.

Remember, your healing isn't just a gift to yourself—it's a beacon for others. It's a beacon that calls to those still lost in the dark, telling them there's a way out, that someone else has walked this path and made it through. And that if I can, perhaps they can too.

THE ISOLATION OF TRAUMA

Trauma is a thief—it steals connection, leaving us isolated from the world, our loved ones, and even ourselves. Research shows that loneliness and isolation have devastating effects on mental and physical health. Studies from institutions like the National Institute on Aging highlight how chronic loneliness increases the risk of depression, anxiety, and even early death. For those who've experienced trauma, the effects are magnified. Trauma teaches us to withdraw, to retreat behind walls we've built to protect ourselves from further pain.

Nowhere is this more evident than in prison. It's a place where so many people who've experienced trauma end up, only to be isolated further. The solution society offers is solitary confinement, locking people away for up to 23 hours a day, often for years on end. The very system that's supposed to reform us only deepens the wounds we carry.

As a teenager in prison, I felt this isolation acutely. Those 23 hours alone in a small cell weren't just lonely—they were soul-crushing. I was already carrying the scars of childhood trauma, and prison compounded them. Sitting in that cell, I built walls around my heart, convinced that if I didn't let anyone in, I couldn't be hurt again.

I struggled to trust others, especially men, who I often saw as threats. I thought keeping my distance would protect me, but in reality, it only kept me stuck. The isolation became a prison within a prison, reinforcing the belief that connection wasn't safe, that I was better off alone.

This disconnection didn't just affect my relationships with others; it seeped into my relationship with myself. I often felt unworthy of love and belonging, convinced that if people saw the real me, they'd walk away. I carried the weight of my pain in silence, and that silence became a prison of its own. The isolation taught me how to numb myself, how to avoid vulnerability at all costs, and how to wear masks that hid the depth of what I was feeling.

By the time I got married and became a father, I had done a lot of work to heal from my past. But trauma has a way of lingering, showing up in small but significant ways. For me, those remnants of pain appeared in moments where I struggled to trust fully or let my guard down completely with my wife or daughters.

Trauma doesn't just isolate individuals—it isolates families. When we're disconnected from ourselves, it's impossible to show up for the people who need us most. I've met men who want to be better husbands and fathers but don't know how, because they're still battling their own demons. They feel the weight of wanting to be there for their families but can't escape the pull of their past.

If this sounds familiar, I want you to know you're not alone. Trauma might make you feel like connection is out of reach, but it's not. Healing is possible, and connection is the bridge that takes us there.

Breaking those walls down isn't easy, but it's worth it. True healing begins when we learn to trust again—trust in others, trust in ourselves, and trust that connection, while risky, is the key to moving forward.

INTIMACY

Intimacy is one of those words we throw around without truly understanding it—until we're confronted with what it really demands. For me, intimacy didn't come naturally. After a childhood of betrayal and pain, letting someone in—*really* in—felt impossible.

When I met Sacha, I had already done some work on myself. I'd faced my past, unravelled some of my pain, and started rebuilding my life. But even with all that progress, I struggled with intimacy in ways I didn't fully understand.

In the beginning, I never knew why I kept pulling away. It wasn't a conscious choice—it was like itchy feet. I couldn't sit still, couldn't relax and enjoy the peaceful moments we shared. Whenever we'd have some quality time together, when everything was calm and beautiful, I'd feel this overwhelming urge to escape.

Thankfully, Sacha, who had completed some training as a therapist, was wise enough to notice. One evening, she gently said, "I've noticed that in these moments, when everything is calm and we get to spend some relaxing time together, you seem like you want to escape. It's like you don't want to be around me. I wonder, is there something going on for you, or have I done something wrong?"

Her words floored me. My first instinct was to jump straight into denial, to tell her, *No, that's not true!* But I held back. I sat with it for a moment and realized she was right. I didn't know why I was trying to escape these beautiful moments, but I promised her I'd try to find out.

I sought out the help of a female therapist called Catherine, and together we quickly uncovered the root of the issue. Everyone close to me in my childhood had hurt me. They lied to me, betrayed me, and made me feel unsafe. That was what I was bumping up against in those moments of closeness with Sacha. When I let her in, I was unconsciously met with the ghosts of my past—the people who had hurt me—and I was terrified she'd do the same.

It was like a lightbulb moment. I couldn't believe it, but there it was. I looked at my therapist and asked, "What do I do now with this? I mean, it's not a pretty picture, is it?"

She smiled and said something that stayed with me: *"I want you to take all of this mess and give it to Sacha. Don't dress it up. Don't try to make it look pretty. Just tell her the truth, because love is big enough to handle this mess."*

I was terrified. I feared Sacha would think I was crazy, or worse, reject me. But I knew I had to try.

I sat her down and told her everything. I said, "Whenever we get close, I'm met with all the people from my childhood who I let get close to me, and who hurt me. And I'm terrified you're going to do the same."

I waited. I braced myself for her to get angry, to shut down, to walk away.

But she didn't.

Instead, she looked at me with tears in her eyes, grabbed my face, and hugged me tightly. Through her tears, she said, "I thought you didn't love me anymore."

I cried into her shoulder, overwhelmed by her compassion and understanding. I told her, "I love you so much. If you hurt me, I don't think my heart would ever recover. This has been my way of trying to protect myself from that. And I'm sorry."

She kissed me and whispered, "I love you too."

I was 30 years old when that happened, and it was my first true experience of intimacy.

That moment changed everything. Intimacy, I realized, isn't about perfection. It's about being honest—showing the parts of yourself you're scared to reveal and trusting that love is big enough to hold them.

Sacha didn't just hear my words; she saw me—the scared boy inside, the man trying so hard to keep it all together. And instead of pulling away, she leaned in.

For those of us who've experienced trauma, intimacy can feel like an impossible ask. But it's also the very thing that heals us. When we let someone in—truly in—it breaks down the walls we've spent a lifetime building and creates space for something new to grow.

That night with Sacha taught me that love isn't just about being loved. It's about being understood. It's about being known. The word *intimacy* can be broken down into an acronym: *into me see.* Letting someone see into me—to see all of me. Not just the pretty and shiny parts, but all the ugly parts too. The pain, the fears, the worries, the insecurities.

True intimacy comes when we allow ourselves to show up as our authentic selves, and for the other person to meet us there—to still love us in that raw, unfiltered state. There is nothing more beautiful than that.

That moment didn't just transform our relationship—it transformed me. It taught me that intimacy isn't a destination; it's a practice. It's about showing up, time and time again, with all of your mess, and trusting that the person you love will meet you there.

FATHERHOOD AND CONNECTION

Becoming a father has changed me in ways I never imagined. It's made me softer, more patient, and more aware of the man I want to be—not just for myself, but for my daughters. Of all the lessons fatherhood has taught me, one moment with my eldest daughter, Sienna, stands out as a turning point.

Sienna was around five years old and hated brushing her teeth. Every night, it was the same battle—me and Sacha taking turns, trying to convince her without forcing her. But no matter what we tried, it always felt like a fight.

One evening, Sienna flat-out refused. She crossed her arms, shouted "No!" and threw her toothbrush across the bathroom. In a split second, something happened. I had a vision of smacking her for being naughty—a flash of frustration and helplessness. Then, just as quickly, another vision followed: me as a little boy, being smacked for far less.

I froze. I caught my breath, stepped back, and walked out of the bathroom. "Can you take over please" I asked Sacha. I knew I wasn't in the right frame of mind.

Later that night, I told Sacha what had happened. "I don't want to be like that," I said. "But I don't know what else to do." In my childhood, the answer to moments like this was always violence. But I didn't want that for my daughters. I knew I needed help.

So, I went back to therapy with Catherine and explained the situation. I told her I needed a solution that wasn't rooted in anger or control. What she said made me laugh at first. "At that age," she explained, "children don't have the emotional ability to process their feelings or communicate what's going on for them, so they act out. It's like a fire—a blazing fire. Your job is to put the fire out. And do you know how you do that? Be the fire blanket."

I looked at her, chuckling to myself and completely confused.

She went on, "Make yourself calm and big. Get down to her eye level, make eye contact, and say, 'I can see you're struggling right now. Would you like a hug?'"

I couldn't help but laugh again. Catherine is Canadian, and I thought, *Maybe this works in Canada where everyone's lovely, but here in the UK? Not a chance.* Still, I decided to try it.

That evening, the usual drama unfolded. Sienna stood in the bathroom, arms crossed, ready for a fight. I got down on my knees, looked her in the eye, and said, "Are you okay, darling? I can see you're struggling right now. Would you like a hug?"

To my complete shock, she stopped. She stared at me for a moment, then ran straight into my arms with such force she nearly knocked me over.

Neither of us said anything. We just stayed there, wrapped in the moment. And then it hit me: connection, right there in the middle of a disagreement. It was something I'd never felt before. Growing up, conflict meant shouting, tears, or worse. The idea that you could find love and connection in the middle of a difficult moment felt impossible.

But here it was. Her small body pressed against mine, her breathing slowing. In that moment, I wasn't just her dad—I was her safe place.

Eventually, she pulled back, looked up at me with a cheeky smile, and I said, "Why don't you show me how you brush your teeth like a big girl?"

To my utter amazement, she picked up the toothbrush and started brushing her teeth with so much enthusiasm it was like she'd just discovered a new favourite toy. Sacha came to the doorway and watched, her jaw practically on the floor. We both stood there in disbelief, marvelling at the transformation.

Later that night, as Sacha and I lay in bed, we talked about what had happened. I found myself getting emotional—not just because the technique had worked, but because of what it meant.

I thought about the little boy I once was. The boy who never got a hug, who never had someone kneel down and say, "I see your really struggling." That moment with Sienna wasn't just about her—it was about me too.

That moment wasn't just a parenting win. It was a reminder of the power of connection, even in the middle of conflict. It's something I'll carry with me forever.

TRUST: THE FOUNDATION OF CONNECTION

Trust is the foundation of any real connection, but if you've been hurt by someone you loved or depended on, it can feel impossible to rebuild. When trust is broken—through betrayal, neglect, or harm—it leaves a mark. It shapes how you see the world and how you let others in.

I know this feeling all too well. Growing up, the people who should have protected me were often the ones who caused me the most pain. By the time I met Sean, I had built walls so high and thick that trusting anyone felt impossible.

When Sean offered to help guide me through recovery, I didn't believe him. I thought, *What's his angle? When's he going to let me down?* But Sean had this way about him—calm, steady, and genuine. He didn't push me to trust him all at once. He just showed up, over and over again, until I felt safe enough to take a chance.

At first, I tested him with small things—sharing bits of my story to see how he'd respond. Each time, he met me with kindness. He didn't judge me or try to fix me. He simply listened. And for the first time, I felt what it was like to let someone in without immediately regretting it.

Trusting Sean became the foundation for trusting others. Slowly, I began to let more people in—first my therapist, then friends in the recovery community, and eventually, Sacha. Each time, it was a risk, and I'll be honest—it didn't always work out.

Not everyone honoured my trust. Some people let me down, and it hurt. But here's the difference now: I'm not the same person I was when those walls first went up. Back then, every betrayal felt like a personal failure, proof that I was unworthy or unlovable. Now, I see it differently.

As an adult, I've learned tools to help me process those moments when trust is broken. I can sit with the disappointment, name the emotions it brings up, and decide what to do next. I've learned that someone letting me down doesn't mean I'm broken or unworthy—it just means they weren't the right person to hold my trust. And that's okay.

When trust is broken, it's easy to stay stuck in a place of hypervigilance, always scanning for threats, always waiting for the next betrayal. But living that way shuts you off from the connection you so desperately need. Rebuilding trust isn't about diving in blindly—it's about taking small steps, little by little, until you feel safe again.

With Sacha, trust wasn't built in one grand moment. It came through small choices, day by day. I'd share a thought, a fear, or a piece of my past, and I'd watch how she responded. Every time she met me with love instead of rejection, a tiny part of my wall came down. Over time, those small moments added up, and I realized she wasn't going to hurt me, lie to me, or leave me.

That's the thing about trust—it's built like bricks, one at a time. And yes, it's a risk. People will hurt you. That's the reality. But the key is knowing that you can handle it. You're no longer the scared child who had no tools or support to process betrayal. Now, as an adult, you have resources. You have people you can turn to, practices to help you navigate your emotions, and the ability to decide what's next.

Trust doesn't mean ignoring red flags or giving everyone a chance. It's about letting the right people in—the ones who will love and support you as you are. It's about dipping your toe in, testing the waters, and knowing you can step back if you need to.

The flipside of trust is discernment. Growing up in the environments I did gave me a sense of judgment that might be more heightened than others. I won't lie—I scan every single adult that comes into my children's lives because of what I experienced as a child. That's not paranoia; that's protection. So when I talk about trust, I'm not talking about blind faith in humanity. I'm asking for a good level of discernment—the ability to judge well. Trust and discernment go hand in hand, and together, they allow us to let people in while still keeping ourselves and our loved ones safe.

HELPING OTHERS

One of the most powerful ways I've discovered connection is through helping others. Trauma often isolates us, convincing us that no one could possibly understand what we've been through. It locks us inside our pain, making us feel like we're carrying it alone. But something extraordinary happens when we step into a space where we're supporting someone else—whether it's mentoring, volunteering, or simply being there for someone we care about. That belief in our aloneness begins to fade. Slowly but surely, we start to see that we're not alone at all.

In my work, I've witnessed the transformative power of this firsthand. I've seen men and women in prison sit across from someone who truly understands their pain—someone who has walked the same path. In those moments, you can see the light flicker in their eyes, the sense of being understood, of being seen. That connection builds a bridge, one that turns shared pain into shared hope, isolation into belonging.

Helping others doesn't just connect us with the world— it gives our pain a purpose. It reminds us that everything we've been through, as dark and difficult as it might have been, can serve as a lifeline for someone else.

But here's what I've learned: this process can't be rushed. Helping others is deeply meaningful, but it has to come at the right time. If you're still navigating the early stages of your own healing journey, it's important to honour where you are. You don't have to rush out and try to save the world just yet. Instead, you can start small—maybe by being there for someone close to you as a person they can talk to. Sometimes, just offering a listening ear is enough to plant the seed of connection for both of you.

This beautiful burden isn't always easy to carry. Sometimes, it means sitting with someone else's pain and resisting the urge to fix it—simply holding space for them to feel seen and heard. Other times, it means sharing your story in a way that allows them to see what's possible for their own lives. Every time we embrace this responsibility, we strengthen our connection to our own journey.

The science supports this too. A study published in *Frontiers in Psychology* found that people who use their painful experiences to help others often report feeling happier, more purposeful, and more at peace with their own past. Helping others doesn't just heal them—it heals us too. It transforms our pain into something meaningful, something that drives us forward and reminds us that our stories are worth sharing.

I've felt this in my own life. When I share my story, when I sit with someone who is struggling, something shifts inside me. It reminds me of the journey I've walked and the lessons I've learned along the way. It connects me to my own humanity and strengthens my resolve to keep showing up—not just for others, but for myself too.

This, I've come to believe, is how we honour the pain we've endured—by turning it into light for someone else. Through helping others, we embody the change we've worked so hard to create within ourselves. And in doing so, we find connection in its most profound form.

That is the beautiful burden. It's not easy, and it's not something to rush into. But when the time is right, it's worth every step.

RECONNECTING TO THE NATURAL WORLD

Painful life experiences have a way of shrinking our world. It narrows our focus, making us hyper-aware of threats and leaving little room for joy, curiosity, or exploration. The world can feel small, heavy, and even dangerous. But as we commit to the work of healing, something profound begins to shift. Slowly, we start to widen our perspective, to see beyond the pain, and reconnect with the beauty and possibility that have always been there, waiting for us.

For me, this reconnection has come through creating new experiences—things I would never have considered before beginning my journey. One of the most transformative practices I've taken up is cold water therapy. Swimming in the sea or a lake, even in the depths of winter, has become a grounding ritual for me. At first, the idea seemed uncomfortable—why would anyone willingly jump into freezing water? But something happens the moment you immerse yourself. The cold shocks your system, demanding your full attention. It forces you to breathe deeply, anchoring you firmly in the present moment. Cold water therapy stimulates the vagus nerve and helps regulate the nervous system. Studies have shown that this practice can significantly reduce symptoms of PTSD, anxiety, and depression, offering a powerful pathway to healing and emotional balance. For me, it's been a way to connect with nature and my body and mind in a way that feels both cleansing and invigorating.

Reconnecting with the natural world has also meant slowing down and finding joy in nature. Gardening has been a surprising source of peace for me. There's something deeply healing about planting a tree, nurturing it, and watching it grow. It's a reminder of the cycles of life—of patience, growth, and renewal. Research backs this up too: studies have shown that gardening can reduce symptoms of PTSD by lowering cortisol levels and improving overall mental health. The simple act of digging in the soil, feeling the earth in your hands, and seeing the fruits of your labour is profoundly grounding.

Beekeeping has been another unexpected blessing in my life. Caring for bees has taught me so much about harmony, community, and the interconnectedness of all living things. There's a calming rhythm to tending to a hive, one that requires focus and presence. Studies suggest that beekeeping can improve overall mental health by reducing stress and promoting mindfulness. For me, it's been a way to connect with something greater than myself, to feel a sense of purpose and stewardship that brings balance to my life.

What I've learned through these experiences is that the things that once felt uncomfortable or out of reach can become sources of joy and connection when we've done the work to heal. Trauma often convinces us to avoid discomfort, to stick with what feels safe. But healing invites us to step into the unfamiliar. It encourages us to revisit old passions we might have abandoned and to try new things we once dismissed.

Science supports the power of creating new experiences in the healing process. Studies show that trying new activities and stepping outside our comfort zones can help rewire the brain, creating fresh neural pathways that reduce the impact of trauma. Whether it's cold water therapy, gardening, beekeeping, or something entirely different, these experiences offer us a way to reengage with the natural world, to feel alive again.

Reconnecting with the natural world doesn't mean forgetting who we are or what we have been through—it means choosing to move forward in spite of it.

CONNECTION TO SOURCE

There have been moments in my life where I should have died. Moments where everything should have ended or come crashing down. Like the time I was cut down in the early hours of the morning, hanging from the bars of my prison cell. I often ask myself—was that just luck? Or was that God? Maybe it's all just coincidence... but maybe coincidence is just God's way of staying anonymous. All I know is, something shifted in those moments, and I felt held by something greater than myself. I call it God—some call it Source, others call it the Universe, Spirit, Creator, or Mother Nature. Whatever name you give it, I believe that energy is always around us, waiting to be noticed. For me, this connection has been a lifeline. It's been fractured at times, especially when my old beliefs about religion got in the way, but it's still there—steady and real. And I feel it strongest when I'm standing by the sea or walking through a forest, not when I'm sitting in a church. So, if life feels heavy, I encourage you to find your own way of connecting to something bigger than yourself. It's a safe place to come home to when the world feels overwhelming.

REFLECTIONS AND INVITATION TO CONNECT

If trauma has left you feeling isolated, I want you to know this: you are not alone. This chapter has been about one of the most profound elements of healing: **connection**. It's the antidote to isolation, the bridge that takes us from loneliness and pain to love and belonging. Connection isn't just about being loved—it's about being seen, heard and understood.

We've explored how difficult life experiences isolate us, cutting us off from others, ourselves, and even the natural world. But more importantly, we've seen how reconnection can transform everything. Through moments of trust, intimacy, and vulnerability—whether it's kneeling down to offer Sienna a hug during a meltdown or sharing my deepest fears with Sacha—we break the cycles that have held us back for so long.

These small but brave acts of connection ripple outward. They change how we show up for our families, our communities, and even ourselves. Connection isn't about diving in all at once; it's about taking those first, courageous steps. Maybe it's sending a message to someone you've lost touch with, saying hello to a neighbour, or sharing a smile with a stranger. These moments, as small as they seem, lead us back to ourselves and to the people who matter most.

And here's the beauty of connection: it not only transforms us but also inspires others. When we live differently—when we dare to trust, to love, and to be seen—we raise the consciousness of those around us. This is how cycles are broken, how generational patterns shift, and how we create a better world.

As you close this chapter, reflect on the moments of connection in your own life. Who are the people who've seen you, supported you, and loved you? Where have you shown up for others? What's one small step you can take today toward connection?

These reflections prepare us for what's next: *Integration and Moving Forward*. In the next chapter, we'll bring together everything you've learned so far—turning these lessons into daily practices that help you create a life filled with meaning, purpose, and peace.

Connection is the ultimate act of showing up—not just for others but for yourself. So, take that step, knock boldly on the door of connection, and trust that the world is waiting for you to let others in.

CHAPTER 6

INTEGRATION AND MOVING FORWARD

IT'S TIME

I never imagined a life like the one I live today. Growing up on a council estate in Isleworth, with neighbours above, below, and on either side of me, my world felt small. The sound of arguments through thin walls, the smell of damp in the air, and the constant reminder that money was tight—that was my normal.

Back then, I couldn't envision anything beyond survival. A life where I'd one day own my own home? Where I'd wake up in a safe, loving space I'd created for my wife and children? It felt impossible.

But here I am.

My home now is filled with laughter, the patter of little feet, and the smell of something delicious coming from the kitchen. It's a place where my daughters feel safe to be themselves, where they're free to play, to laugh, to cry—without fear. It's a place where my wife, Sacha, and I sit together in the evenings, grateful for what we've built.

This home isn't just bricks and mortar. It's a symbol of the life I never thought was possible.

Because let's be honest: the odds weren't in my favour. I didn't have any qualifications. I carried the weight of trauma, addiction, and a criminal past. I wasn't the kind of man anyone expected to succeed. And yet, here I am—a sober man, a husband, a father, a business owner, a charity founder, and even an award-winning author.

How did I get here? It wasn't luck, and it wasn't handed to me. It was a decision—a choice to take responsibility for my life and do the work to change it.

Let me tell you something I've learned along the way: when you decide to change your life, doubt and fear will show up. They'll whisper all the reasons why you can't do it, why it's too late, or why you're not capable. But here's the truth: the answer to creating the life you dream of lies in one place—it's you. It's always been you.

Taking responsibility for your life is one of the most powerful decisions you'll ever make. It's the moment you realize that no one is coming to save you. No one else can fight your battles or carry your burdens. While support and guidance are vital, it's up to you to show up, to do the work, and to create the change.

This isn't about blaming yourself for the past. It's not about shame or self-criticism. It's about reclaiming your power. It's about recognizing that no matter how painful your story has been, you hold the pen now. You are the author, and every new day is a blank page waiting for you to write something extraordinary.

I'm sharing this because I know how easy it is to feel stuck, to believe that the life you want is out of reach. But I promise you, it's not. If I can come from where I did and create a life like this, so can you.

Here's what I want you to know: you carry a unique gift—a purpose that only you can bring into this world. That gift isn't just for you; it's for the lives you will touch, the people you will inspire, and the change you will create.

This won't be easy, and it shouldn't be. Growth demands courage, discipline, and resilience. But every time you rise above your doubts, push through your fears, and lean into this work, you're not just transforming your life—you're creating ripples that will touch others.

I know because I've lived it.

The world I grew up in and the world I live in now are night and day. The bridge between them wasn't a magic trick—it was a decision, followed by consistent action.

In this chapter, I'm going to share some of the tools that helped me truly integrate everything I've been through, move forward, and create the life I truly deserve.

It's time.

GO ALL IN

Change doesn't happen by dipping your toes in the water—it requires a leap of faith. Half-hearted efforts lead to half-hearted results. If you truly want to transform your life, you have to be brave, be courageous, and put yourself out there fearlessly.

I remember hearing a quote during a training course with Tony Robbins back in 2007, just after I got sober: "If you want to take the island, burn the boats." That stuck with me. It means there's no turning back, no plan B. When you commit fully—when you remove any possibility of retreat—you unlock a level of focus and determination you didn't even know you had.

For me, going all in started at 25, when I decided to get sober and go to AA. Back in 2007, being sober wasn't something to shout about or be proud of. If you went to AA at 25, you weren't seen as brave or strong—you were seen as a bum, a loser, a nobody. And yet, I knew I couldn't live the way I was anymore. My mindset had to be all or nothing. Either I was fully committed to change, or I wasn't. That's what going all in looked like for me. And yes, today, sobriety is more supported, even looked at as cool in some circles, but back then, it wasn't like that. It took everything in me to show up and say, *I'm ready to change.*

When we show up fully, when we give everything we've got, something magical happens. It's as though the universe hears the song we're playing and responds in kind. People, opportunities, and resources start to appear as if by design, aligning to help us on our journey. This isn't just luck—it's the power of commitment. The energy you put out is reflected back to you.

I've seen this play out time and time again in my own life. The moment I stopped playing it safe, the moment I decided to give everything to my recovery, my relationships, and my purpose, doors began to open. Whether it was meeting the right mentors, finding the courage to start a business, or even connecting with my wife—it all began with a decision to go all in.

So that's what I'm calling in for you. Be brave enough to burn the boats. Don't leave yourself an easy way out or a plan B. Commit fully to the change you want to see in your life. It's not easy, and it's not comfortable, but it's worth it.

POVERTY MINDSET VS. SUCCESS MINDSET

When it comes to creating a meaningful life, everything begins with your mindset. A poverty mindset clings to fear, excuses, and self-doubt. It convinces you that you're not enough, that life is stacked against you, and that it's safer to stay where you are than to risk failure. It's a mindset rooted in scarcity—believing that time, resources, and opportunities are limited. This belief system traps you in a cycle of stagnation, finding every reason not to take the leap, not to try, and ultimately, not to succeed.

I know this mindset all too well—because it used to be mine. I had every excuse lined up as to why I couldn't make something of my life. My mum was an Irish immigrant with no formal education. Neither of my parents could read or write. I'd been to prison. I'd failed at school. I had no qualifications. I was an addict. I'd suffered deep trauma as a child. The list went on, and for a long time, I let it define me. I let those reasons convince me that a better life wasn't possible.

But the truth is, none of that changes until you decide it does. Nobody was coming to save me. Nobody was going to hand me the life I wanted. Remembering what I said earlier, Who is going to change it? The answer is me. No one else. Radical ownership. Ownership over my own life. It wasn't easy, but I started to shift from a poverty mindset to a success mindset. Instead of focusing on the reasons why I couldn't, I began asking myself, How can I?

A success mindset isn't about having all the answers; it's about finding them. It's about *resourcefulness*. It's about refusing to let fear and excuses hold you back. I burned my boats—I gave myself no way to retreat, no way to fall back into old patterns. Instead, I moved forward with courage, trusting that action would lead to opportunities, and it did. The right people, resources, and circumstances began to appear, but only because I showed up for my life with unwavering determination.

This is the mindset shift that changes everything. It's about moving from scarcity to abundance, from excuses to action. Success doesn't care about your past or your circumstances. It belongs to those who refuse to quit, who own their story, and who dare to believe that they can create something better.

So, ask yourself: Are you ready to own your life? To take radical ownership for your future? To stop finding reasons why you can't and start finding ways that you can? The choice is yours. It always has been. And it always will be.

TIME TO SHINE

You didn't come this far, face your pain, and heal all them old wounds just to play small. The work you've done—

the lessons, the breakthroughs, the transformation—has shaped you into someone unique. Someone with gifts only you can bring into the world. Only you have lived your exact experiences. Only you have your story, your perspective, your voice. And those gifts aren't just for you—they're meant to touch others, to help those who need what only you can offer.

This is your time. Your time to integrate all that you've learned, to embody the wisdom you've gained, and to show the world what's possible when we commit to change. It's not just about living your life; it's about owning it. You've earned the right to live boldly, with purpose and passion, and to step fully into the person you were always meant to be.

This work is bigger than you. The struggles you've faced and overcome have given you a unique ability to reach people who are still in the darkness. The lessons you've learned are the lifeline someone else is searching for. Maybe they're walking the same path you once were—lost, hurting, and convinced they can't make it. But your life, your story, your courage can be the evidence they need to believe change is possible.

So, step into it fully. Trust that the lessons you've integrated and the light you've cultivated will draw the right people, opportunities, and experiences into your life.

THE IMPORTANCE OF AIMING HIGH

As you step into the next phase of your journey, I want to emphasise this: Aim high. Don't settle for mediocrity or what feels "good enough." You've done the hard work of healing, growing, and transforming your life—now it's time to aim for the extraordinary. When we aim high, we challenge ourselves to reach beyond what we think is possible, expanding our vision of who we are and what we're capable of.

I learned this powerful lesson when I was working with my business coach, Donnie, in London. One day, he asked me to set a goal that felt almost impossible. At first, I hesitated, thinking, *What's the point?* But then I said it out loud: "I want to retire by the time I'm 40."

It felt ridiculous, like an unreachable dream. But Donnie didn't flinch. He encouraged me to go for it, to create a plan and take bold, deliberate steps toward that vision. That moment was the start of something bigger—a journey that taught me the value of setting ambitious goals and taking the small, necessary steps to make them happen.

Retiring at 35 didn't happen by chance. It happened because I surrounded myself with the right people, built good systems, and made intentional choices. I invested in the best coaches, like Donnie, who helped me see what was possible. I focused on recruiting the right staff, people who shared my vision and could run the business with integrity and competence. I learned how to manage my money wisely, investing in opportunities that would secure my family's future.

My circle of friends also changed. I began spending time with people who challenged and inspired me, people who were building something meaningful in their own lives. Their influence kept me focused and motivated, showing me what was possible when you align yourself with the right energy.

Every part of the journey—coaching, systems, staff, investments, friendships—played a role in making that dream a reality. And by the time I was 35—five years ahead of schedule—I had stepped away from my business, living the life I had once only dared to dream of in Devon.

The lesson here isn't just about retiring early; it's about understanding that big goals require both vision and action. You don't have to know exactly how you'll get there, but you do have to start. Surround yourself with the right people, take small, consistent steps, and trust that every action you take is moving you closer to the life you want.

This is the power of aiming high. Studies consistently show that setting ambitious goals leads to greater achievement, motivation, and life satisfaction. Aiming high doesn't mean you'll never face failure—it means you're willing to dream big and take bold steps, knowing that even if you fall short of the goal, the process will transform you. It's not about perfection; it's about growth.

When we aim high, we set a new standard for our lives. It shifts our perspective and reminds us that we're capable of more than we imagined. This mindset not only drives us forward but inspires those around us to aim higher too. On the other hand, aiming low might feel safe, but it limits growth, breeds complacency, and reinforces the belief that we're not capable of more.

If you aim for *nothing*, you'll hit it every time. But when you dare to aim high, you unlock the potential within yourself to achieve far more than you ever thought possible. So dream boldly, act courageously, and trust that aiming high will take you further than you can imagine. This is your invitation to reach for greatness.

VISUALISATION: THE POWER OF SEEING YOUR FUTURE

Back in 2012 when I first set up Oakhill, still navigating a world that felt both daunting and full of possibility, I was introduced to a tool that would profoundly shape my journey: the vision board. My business coach, Donnie, encouraged me to visualize the life I wanted, even though it seemed like a distant dream. In my mum's spare room, I assembled a vision board with images of a beautiful home, a loving family, and symbols of stability and success—things I yearned for but scarcely believed I could achieve.

I placed pictures that represented my deepest desires—a home with a stunning view, a happy couple walking down the aisle, a family together on the beach, a Range Rover, and a robust bank balance. These weren't just idle dreams; they were beacons toward a future I desperately wanted to realize.

Having grown up in poverty, I didn't want my children to experience the constant stress and worry of where our next meal was coming from. I wanted to create a life of comfort and stability—a home we owned, a place where no landlord or council could evict us. These weren't just material goals; they were about providing security, something I'd rarely known growing up.

Donnie urged me to believe in the possibility of these dreams, to hold onto them, and to let them guide my actions. He showed me that it wasn't just about wishing for a better life—it was about taking deliberate steps toward building it. And as the years passed, those steps began to add up, slowly turning dreams into reality.

Fast forward to December 15th, 2017, a day that will always be one of the most meaningful of my life. It was the day everything seemed to come full circle in ways I never could have imagined.

That morning, I got a call from the solicitors confirming the completion date for our new home in Devon. The date? December 15th. At first, I didn't register the significance, but then it hit me—it was my ten-year sobriety anniversary. I couldn't believe it. The house wasn't just any house either. It was *the house*—the one I had visualized years before. It had the view I'd once cut out and placed on my old vision board, a beacon of hope when I was just starting out, trying to build a life I could be proud of.

What made this even more surreal was learning from the solicitors that, in a chain of fifteen people—spanning from those moving out of a one-bedroom flat in Clapham to us moving into our dream home in Devon—everyone had agreed on the same completion date: December 15th. The odds of that alignment felt astronomical, as though the universe itself had orchestrated the timing. It was a powerful affirmation of my journey, a reminder of how far I had come.

Later that day, surrounded by family and friends at the Richmond Hill Hotel in Surrey, I proposed to Sacha—my long-term partner and the mother of my children. My heart raced as I got down on one knee. This was the woman who had stood by me, believed in me, and been part of every step of this journey. When she said yes, the room erupted into cheers, filling the space with love and joy. It felt like life was giving me the most incredible gift—a moment that was as much about celebrating us as it was about the journey we'd walked together.

And then, a few weeks later as I unpacked boxes in our new home, I stumbled across my old vision board. As I looked at the pictures on it, one detail stopped me in my tracks. The Range Rover I had once imagined owning had a number plate with the number ten—echoing my decade of sobriety and the significance of the 15th of December. Seeing that detail, I was struck by the power of visualization.

Looking back, what amazes me most is how much of that vision board came to life. At the time I made it, it felt like a distant dream, something almost impossible. But I held onto it. I worked toward it, step by step, often not knowing how or if it would happen. And yet, here I was— living the dream I had dared to imagine.

This experience reminded me of the importance of holding a vision. It's not about magical thinking or expecting the universe to do all the work. It's about keeping the image of what you want in your mind and taking deliberate, consistent action toward it. Visualization isn't just about dreaming—it's about believing in the possibility and putting in the effort to make it real.

December 15th wasn't just a day of celebration for me—it was a reminder of how far I'd come, how powerful a clear vision can be, and how beautiful life can become when you align your actions with your dreams.

The science behind visualization supports its efficacy. Mental rehearsals can activate the same neural pathways as physical actions, helping your brain to start working as if your dreams are already unfolding. This not only builds confidence but also primes you to seize opportunities that align with your goals.

I'll admit, even now, it feels a bit funny talking about this. There's something about the whole idea that feels a little like magic, doesn't it? You cut out a few pictures, stick them on a board, and somehow life starts aligning in ways you never expected. But here's the thing—it works. As strange as it sounds, when you visualize something clearly and back it up with action, things start to shift. It's not magic in the traditional sense, but it can feel that way when the pieces start falling into place.

If you're standing where I once was, fresh out of chaos and full of doubt, or if you're simply seeking a change, let me offer this piece of advice: dare to visualize. Dare to dream big. It doesn't matter how distant it seems. Gather images that inspire you, place them where you can see them every day, and allow them to fuel your journey forward.

Remember, visualizing your future isn't a passive act. It's not about cutting out pictures, sitting back, and waiting for the universe to deliver a Range Rover to your driveway. It's a robust strategy for life-building. It requires not just the dream but also the willingness to take daily actions toward making those dreams a reality. As it's said, "Ask, and it shall be given you; seek, and ye shall find; knock, and it shall be opened unto you" (Matthew 7:7). By visualizing, you're knocking on the door of your future, boldly asking for what you want, and preparing yourself to step through when the opportunity arises.

The life I once thought impossible is now my reality—a testament to the power of dreaming big and showing up every day to make those dreams a reality. And listen, if I can turn pictures on a vision board into the life I live today, you can do this too. So, what does the life you truly want look like? Don't hold back. Go big. And then show up every day, ready to make it happen.

COACHING AND THERAPY: NAVIGATING THE PATH FORWARD

If you'd told me years ago that I'd be sitting here, singing the praises of therapy and coaching, I would have laughed you out of the room. Growing up, I thought therapy was for nutjobs and that the only people who had coaches were professional boxers. Therapy? Not for me. Coaches? Only if you were stepping into the ring. The idea of sitting down and talking about my feelings with a stranger felt ridiculous. I thought I could figure it all out on my own. Spoiler alert: I couldn't.

Fast forward to today, and I can confidently say that therapy and coaching have been two of the most transformative tools in my journey. Without them, I honestly don't know if I'd be where I am now. Therapy, in particular, plays a vital role at this stage of the journey—one of integration and moving forward. It's not just about healing old wounds but also about providing a support system to help navigate life as you step into a new version of yourself.

Therapy is especially valuable here because it helps identify blind spots and old patterns that might creep back in. We've all had moments where we slip into behaviours or ways of thinking we thought we'd left behind. Therapy acts as a safeguard, helping to recognize and address these moments before they pull us back to where we started. It's about staying on course and continuing to grow.

Since 2007, I've worked with a variety of therapists and coaches, each bringing their own unique approach to my life. Some challenged me to look at things from angles I'd never considered. Others provided me with practical tools to stay grounded and focused. Each one has left an imprint on my journey, and I'm grateful for the wisdom and support they've offered along the way.

So, here's my advice to you: if you're serious about growth and self development, find yourself a therapist or coach. Look for someone who can challenge you, guide you, and reflect back the parts of yourself you might not yet see. The value of that kind of relationship is hard to put into words, but it's one of the most powerful tools you'll ever have.

Therapy and coaching aren't about "fixing" what's broken. They're about fostering a deeper understanding of yourself, unlocking your potential, and equipping you with the tools to create a life that feels meaningful and fulfilled. And yes, it takes commitment—not just time or money, but a commitment to yourself and your own future.

So, if you're standing at a crossroads, unsure of your next step, consider this: could a therapist or coach help you get back on track?

GRIEF IS A PROCESS

If you find yourself grieving, I want you to know that it's okay. Grief is not a setback—it's part of the process of healing. It's a natural, sacred response to loss and an essential step on this journey of integration and moving forward.

Grief is a process—a deeply human, deeply necessary process. And yet, so many of us misunderstand it. We avoid it, suppress it, or push it aside, thinking it's something to "get over" or "move past." But what if grief is something far more sacred?

I remember sitting with a wise Lakota elder who shared a story that transformed how I see grief. He spoke of how, in their tradition, grief was not something to be feared or hidden away—it was a gift, a bridge between worlds.

He told me that when someone in their community passed on, their loved ones would cry not out of despair but as an act of love. Those tears, he explained, were seen as fuel to help their loved one's soul find safe passage back to the Creator, back to the ancestors who had gone before them.

He looked me in the eye and said something I'll never forget: *"Grief is praise. It is love's way of understanding the loss of something you cherished."*

Man, those words hit me deep. They reshaped not only the way I see grief but also the way I see love.

You see, as we arrive at this stage of our journey—where we've stopped numbing our emotions with alcohol, drugs, or distractions—we begin to welcome all parts of ourselves, including the sadness of what was lost. Grief becomes something we no longer suppress, because we understand it as a natural and sacred part of the human experience.

It's okay to grieve. In fact, it's necessary. I often shed tears myself, whether I'm witnessing someone else's process or sitting in the middle of a sweat lodge ceremony, feeling the weight of my own losses. Those tears aren't a sign of weakness—they're a way of honouring what was, of celebrating the depth of what I've loved and lost.

The Lakota saw grief as something natural, something to be embraced rather than avoided. They didn't rush it or try to fix it. They made space for it, understanding that grief is as much a part of life as love itself. I hope that one day, we in the West can begin to see grief the same way—not as something to push through, but as something to honour.

So how does grief tie into integration and moving forward?

When we grieve, we are integrating. We're taking the emotions, the memories, and the pain of what we've lost and finding a place for them in our story. Grief allows us to reconcile the past with the present. It helps us acknowledge what was, honour what it meant, and begin to move forward with those lessons and love intact.

Grief is not a wall that keeps us stuck; it's a bridge that helps us cross into the next chapter of our lives. It's through grieving that we make peace with what's behind us, so we can carry its meaning forward without being weighed down by its pain.

Integration is about wholeness. It's about making room for every part of our experience—the joy, the pain, the love, the loss—and weaving them together into something that feels complete. Grief is a vital thread in that tapestry.

As we grieve, we're not just letting go of the past—we're celebrating it, honouring it, and allowing it to shape us into someone who can move forward with strength, wisdom, and love. Grief is not the end of the story; it's a part of the journey that makes us whole.

So, if you find yourself grieving, remember this: it's not a step backward. It's a step toward healing. It's a part of integration, a way of honouring the depth of your love and the importance of your experiences. It's how we move forward—not by leaving the past behind, but by carrying its meaning with us into the future.

WHEN THINGS GET HARD

Life, as we know it, has a way of testing us, especially when we're striving to change our paths. There will be moments when it seems as if the whole world is against us, when the weight of our past, our present struggles, or even the whispers of our own doubts feel just too heavy to bear. I've been there, in those deep valleys of despair, and I want to share this with you because I know I'm not alone in these experiences.

I remember distinctly the days and nights spent in a prison cell as a teenager. The cold, grey walls felt like they were closing in on me. It was as if I had ruined everything, with no way out of the chaos I'd created for myself. Shame was my constant companion, telling me this was all I was meant to be. And for a long time, I believed it.

Yet, in that darkness, there was a faint glimmer—a quiet voice that seemed almost a whisper amid the storm. It said, *This doesn't have to be your end.* It wasn't a loud, confident proclamation. It didn't outline a clear path forward or promise an easy journey. It simply reminded me that change was possible, that I wasn't doomed to stay stuck.

That tiny spark didn't change my circumstances overnight. It didn't undo the past or the consequences waiting for me. But it gave me something crucial—a sliver of hope to cling to. Slowly, I started to believe in the possibility of a better life. That belief became my lifeline, my reason to keep pushing forward, one day at a time.

This journey of change, I learned, is deeply personal and filled with challenges. It's a path you must walk yourself. While there will be wonderful people who will offer you support and encouragement, ultimately, no one can take the steps for you. You are the one who must rise every time you fall. You are the one who has to persevere when it feels like the whole world is against you.

But here's another truth I've come to know: **you are capable**. And part of that capability involves embracing radical ownership—being the captain of your own ship. It's about owning your past, your mistakes, your victories, and your course. It means taking responsibility for your life, for every part of it, and making the necessary changes to steer toward a better future.

Think of the countless individuals who have risen from the depths of unimaginable circumstances to achieve remarkable things. Viktor Frankl, who found meaning in the despair of a concentration camp. Nelson Mandela, who emerged from 27 years in prison to lead a nation towards unity and forgiveness. J.K. Rowling, who transformed her life from being a single mother on welfare to becoming one of the most celebrated authors of our time. Their stories are not just narratives of success; they are beacons of human resilience and determination. They took ownership of their fates and changed their stories.

When the road gets tough—as it inevitably will—it's okay to feel overwhelmed, scared, or even ready to give up. But in those moments, remember the stories of those who have walked this path before you.

And if you ever find yourself on the brink of giving up, whether it's on your marriage, your family, or any part of your life that once felt right, pause and ask yourself a few hard questions: Have you truly done all you can? Have you tried to connect on a deeper level? Have you really explored every possible avenue for healing and reconciliation?

Sharing this is essential for me, as someone who came from a broken home where a predator found an easy way in. It's a story I hear all too often in the work I do, and the statistics back it up. Children from broken homes are disproportionately likely to face incarceration, commit crimes, suffer abuse, or struggle with addiction.

So when life tests you, when things get really hard, I urge you to dig deep. Do the work necessary to change your story. Embrace radical ownership of your life. Your future self will thank you for not giving up too soon, for not walking away before the miracle happens. Remember, the most challenging battles often lead to the most cherished victories.

REFLECTIONS AND ENCOURAGEMENTS

Now, before you roll your eyes or think, *Here we go, another self-help guru trying to sell me the dream,* let me clarify something: I'm not a life coach, a guru, or a saint. I'm just a man who somehow clawed his way back up from the gutter. I've sat in the chaos, lived through the mess, and come out the other side with a few lessons to share.

Honestly, when I first heard about things like visualization, therapy, or radical ownership, I thought it was a load of nonsense. I couldn't wrap my head around how staring at a vision board or talking about my feelings could change anything. But here I am, bloody promoting it. And if you know me, you'll know I wouldn't back anything that hasn't worked for me. So there we go.

This chapter has been about taking everything you've learned and weaving it into the fabric of your life. It's about going all in—no half-hearted efforts—and shifting from scarcity to abundance. It's about using visualization to create your future, embracing therapy or coaching to navigate the hard parts, and most importantly, taking radical ownership of your life.

Radical ownership isn't glamorous. It's not something you can slap on a T-shirt or hashtag your way through. It's messy, humbling, and at times, downright uncomfortable. But it's also liberating. It's the moment you realize that while you can't control everything, you can control your choices—and that's where your power lies.

As we move into the final chapter, *Peace,* I want you to think about what you're working toward. Because peace isn't something you stumble upon one day. It's not like you wake up, and suddenly life is calm, and the birds are chirping on cue. Peace is something you build. It's the result of the work you've done—of showing up, facing the hard truths, and creating a foundation of love and purpose.

So, take a deep breath and prepare yourself for this final step. You've done the work. You've faced the storms. Now it's time to explore what it means to live in peace—with yourself, with others, and with the world around you.

CHAPTER 7

PEACE

"How much peace can you take before you find yourself reaching for the chaos that once felt normal?"

Peace. It's what so many of us crave yet often struggle to hold onto. After a life of chaos, peace can feel foreign—almost like an uninvited guest that doesn't quite belong in the home you've built. But peace isn't just the absence of chaos; it's the final destination of this journey. It's what all the work, the pain, and the breakthroughs have been leading to. And once you find it, the real work begins: protecting it.

This chapter is about not only finding peace but also safeguarding it. It's about learning to recognize when old patterns of self-sabotage try to pull you back into the chaos, whether that chaos comes from the people around you or the habits you've spent years unlearning. Peace can feel uncomfortable at first, especially after a lifetime of trauma and, at times, self-created chaos. Sitting in calm can almost feel like sitting in a void, one that whispers, *"Stir the pot; create some drama—this isn't normal for you."* But the truth is, that feeling of discomfort is your old self calling, and your new self needs to respond differently.

To live in peace, you must resist the urge to go backward, to create chaos because that's what feels familiar. And let me be clear: protecting peace doesn't mean isolating yourself or cutting off the world. It means learning how to say no when something threatens the calm you've worked so hard to cultivate. It means setting boundaries with people who pull you into their storms and learning how to quiet the storm within yourself. Most importantly, it's about recognizing that peace is not just a gift—it's a responsibility.

One of the tools I've found incredibly helpful in maintaining peace is something I call the "one to ten scale." Imagine your emotional state on a scale from one to ten. A "one" represents depression or complete exhaustion, while a "ten" represents elation, overwhelming joy, and excitement. The goal isn't to live at either extreme—it's to aim for somewhere between a five and a seven. That's the sweet spot: calm, consistent, and peaceful.

There will be moments when you venture up to a ten, when joy floods your life, and everything feels perfect. And there will also be times when you drop down to a one, when your depressed or difficulty temporarily takes over. These fluctuations are natural. But the aim is to live most of your life between a five and a seven—a steady, balanced state where peace becomes your baseline.

This scale helps you recognize when you're veering too far into either extreme, whether it's getting swept up in the chaos of a ten or sinking into the despair of a one. It's a simple, practical way to check in with yourself and gently guide your emotions back to centre.

Peace is also about finding something greater than yourself to anchor you in that balance. For some, that might be God. For others, it could be a connection to nature, the universe, or their own inner sense of purpose. Whatever it is, let that connection be your guiding force when the old patterns start creeping in.

Peace isn't just about feeling calm in the moment—it's about building a life where calm becomes your foundation. This chapter will walk you through what it takes to not only live in peace but to make it your new normal. It's about reprogramming your mind and body to accept calm as your default setting and learning how to stay grounded in a world that sometimes feels designed to throw us off balance.

And most importantly, it's about understanding that you deserve this peace. You've earned it, and no one—not even yourself—has the right to take it away.

THE JOURNEY TO PEACE

If you've lived through trauma, chaos can feel like home. It becomes a strange kind of normal, something your brain and body adjust to over time. For so many of us, calm feels unsettling—almost like it's a trick, like something's about to go wrong. This isn't just in your imagination. Trauma rewires the brain, creating a hypervigilant state where you're constantly scanning for danger. It keeps you stuck in fight-or-flight mode, always bracing for the next blow.

The work of finding peace isn't just about creating a calm environment. It's about unlearning what your nervous system has been conditioned to believe. It's about teaching your brain and body that safety is okay, that stillness isn't something to fear, and that calm doesn't mean you're about to lose everything. But here's the hard part: peace doesn't always feel like a reward—it can feel like punishment. If you've spent a lifetime in chaos, part of you might feel like you don't deserve the calm. That inner critic, that old voice, will whisper, "Don't get too comfortable. This won't last."

I've been there. When I moved to Devon, stepping away from the business I had worked so hard to build, I thought I'd made it. I had the home I dreamed of, the time to spend with my family, and the quiet I had craved for years. For a while, I allowed myself to settle into that peace, but then the voice came back—the one I thought I had left behind. "This is too good to be true," it whispered. "Don't get used to it. It could all be taken away."

It's that voice—the one born of trauma—that so many of us carry. It's the voice that convinces us to sabotage the good things in our lives, to stir up chaos because that's what feels normal. And if we're not careful, we'll listen to it. We'll ruin the peace we've fought so hard to create, not because we want to, but because calm feels unfamiliar, and we don't trust it.

But maybe it's not just individual lives where this pattern plays out. As nations, it seems we're addicted to chaos too. Throughout history, war and conflict have been constants, shaping societies and dominating the world stage.

In the last 3,400 years, humans have only known around 268 years of peace—less than 8% of recorded history. The rest of the time, we've been at war with each other, whether over land, power, or ideology.

Even now, in the modern era, conflict is rarely far from the headlines. As nations, we've poured more energy into fighting than into fostering long-term peace. Could this collective addiction to chaos influence us on an individual level? If we live in a world where chaos is normalized— where wars rage on, and violence seems inevitable—is it any wonder that living peacefully feels like a challenge?

The journey to peace isn't just about finding it—it's about learning how to protect it. Individually, this means doing the work to quiet the voices born of trauma, to unlearn the belief that calm is temporary or undeserved. Collectively, it means rethinking how we approach peace, not as a fleeting pause between wars but as a foundation for how we live.

The world reflects the people within it, and maybe, just maybe, if more of us commit to healing our own chaos, we can start to change the larger narrative.

ENERGY VAMPIRES

Not everyone will cheer for your growth. Some people will be drawn to your light, but not to celebrate it—they'll want to dim it. These are the energy vampires, the ones who drain your joy, undermine your progress, and try to pull you back into the patterns you're working so hard to break free from. They thrive in chaos and negativity, and their comfort lies in keeping things exactly as they've always been. If you let them, they'll siphon the energy you've worked so hard to build.

I've experienced this firsthand. When I started my journey of change, I expected those around me to be happy for me, to celebrate my progress. But that wasn't always the case. Some people resisted my growth, not because they hated me, but because my change made them uncomfortable.

I'll never forget a moment back in the early days of setting up my business, Oakhill, in Isleworth. Across the road from my office is a pub called The Castle. One evening, as I walked past, some old friends were outside drinking and smoking weed.

One of them called out, "Yes, Maisey, what's happening?"

I nodded and said, "Alright, mate."

Another chimed in, "Look at you, bro, in your suit. You've changed, man."

I stopped for a second and said, "Yeah, you're right, mate. I have changed. I had to. I was either going to end up dead or doing a life sentence."

They didn't respond. They just looked at me, like my words didn't land.

As I turned to walk away, one of them said, "You still sober, Maisey?"

I nodded, "Yeah."

He shook his head and said, "That's one thing I'll never understand. You never even drank every day. I reckon you've been brainwashed by AA, bruv."

That's when my patience wore thin. I turned back and said, "You're right—I needed my brain washed. It was full of nonsense. And listen to me now, if you lot aren't going to support what I'm doing, at least don't try and tear me down."

One of them kissed their teeth, and another said, "Alright, Maisey, all good, bro."

I walked away that day thinking, *Thank God I'm not sitting in that pub doing the same thing we were doing when we were teenagers.* I felt a surge of pride—not in a smug way, but because I knew how hard I'd worked to get to where I was, and I wasn't about to let anyone drag me back.

Here's the thing: your energy is sacred. If you spend your days surrounded by people who complain, gossip, or resist change, their negativity will seep into you. It's like trying to climb a mountain while stuck in a swamp—you'll never get anywhere. But when you surround yourself with people who lift you up, who challenge you to be better, and who are on their own journeys of growth, your world begins to transform.

Think about it this way: high-energy people don't just motivate you—they hold you accountable to your potential. They remind you of what's possible and inspire you to keep striving for the life you want. They're the kind of people who will celebrate when you're winning, cheering you on with genuine joy, not gossiping behind your back or judging you from the sidelines.

Studies back this up. Research shows that the people we spend the most time with significantly impact our habits, mindsets, and success. If you're surrounded by people striving to grow, that energy will push you to grow too. But if you're constantly around negativity, it will weigh you down.

This isn't about judging others or thinking you're better than anyone. It's about protecting your energy and your peace. It's about being intentional with who you allow into your inner circle.

You wouldn't hand over your wallet to just anyone—so why would you hand over your energy, your time, or your trust?

If you've worked hard to grow, to change, to build something better for yourself, you don't owe anyone anything. Surround yourself with people who celebrate your growth, not those who try to tear it down.

In closing, remember, not everyone is meant to come with you on your journey. And that's okay. Protect your energy, because it's the foundation of everything you're building. And the people who truly support you? They'll walk alongside you, cheering every step of the way.

THE DOOR THAT CLOSES AND THE ONE THAT OPENS

As painful as it is to see old friendships fade or relationships become strained, trust that this is clearing space for something better. When you commit to living in alignment with your true self, the right people—the ones who resonate with your growth and values—will begin to show up.

I know this phase can feel heavy. It's not easy to let go of people you've cared about, especially when you feel guilt creeping in. For a long time, I carried that guilt like a weight on my back. I felt like I owed it to my old friends who were still struggling to stay close to them, to try and help them improve. I believed I could carry us all forward. But the truth is, no matter how much you want it for someone else, they have to want it for themselves.

There were people I cared about deeply who didn't understand the path I was on. My growth made them uncomfortable. It wasn't because they didn't love me—it was because they weren't ready to confront their own struggles. My progress felt like a spotlight on the areas in their lives they weren't ready to address. Letting go of those relationships wasn't easy. But I learned that letting go wasn't abandoning them—it was honouring my own journey.

The tension of this phase—losing old connections while waiting for new ones to form—is one of the clearest indicators that you're levelling up. Growth is never without its challenges, and integration is no exception. But this period of transition is also an opportunity. It's a chance to solidify who you are now, to stand firm in your values, and to let go of anything—or anyone—that's holding you back.

If you're in this space right now, I want you to know that I've been there too. It's uncomfortable, and it hurts. But on the other side of this discomfort are friendships and connections that will enrich your life in ways you can't yet imagine. Your tribe will call. You'll find people who inspire you, support you, and challenge you to keep growing. These are the friendships that feel like coming home, the connections that remind you why you did the work in the first place.

You'll know you've found your tribe when you look around and see people living purposeful, joyful lives. They're not threatened by your growth; they celebrate it. They're not dragging you backward; they're walking alongside you, building something meaningful together. These are the people who lift you up when you falter, who hold space for your dreams, and who remind you of what's possible when you live in alignment with your true self.

So, if you find yourself in this tricky space, take heart. It's not the end of the story; it's the beginning of a new chapter. Trust that the discomfort of this moment is temporary and that what's waiting on the other side is worth it.

I'm living proof of that. The friendships I have now—built on trust, purpose, and mutual respect—are some of the most beautiful and enriching connections I've ever known. They wouldn't have been possible if I hadn't been willing to let go of what no longer served me.

PROTECTING YOUR PEACE THROUGH BOUNDARIES

For years, I didn't know how to set boundaries. I'd let people take more than I could give, ignoring the resentment and exhaustion building up inside me. I thought being a "good" person meant always being available, always saying yes, and always putting others first. It wasn't until I began healing that I realized how unsustainable—and unhealthy—that way of living was.

Boundaries aren't about keeping people out—they're about keeping yourself safe. They're about knowing your limits and respecting them, even if others don't. Setting boundaries is an act of self-love, but for me, it's also an act of love for my family.

When Sacha and I moved to Devon, it was one of the biggest boundary-setting decisions I've ever made. Leaving London's hustle and stepping away from relationships and habits that no longer served me wasn't easy. Some people didn't understand, and some even felt hurt. But I knew I needed to create space for myself, for my family, and for the peace we were working so hard to build.

Protecting that peace means saying no to things that drain me, prioritizing the practices that keep me grounded, and creating an environment where my family feels safe, loved, and connected.

Boundaries don't always have to be enforced with force. Most of the time, they come from gentle communication or slowly detaching and letting go with love. It might be as simple as saying, "I'm not available for that right now," or deciding not to engage with someone who drains your energy. It's not about building walls—it's about choosing what and who you let into your space.

Here are some ways to start:

1. Get Clear on Your Non-Negotiables

Take time to reflect on what truly matters to you—your values, priorities, and the practices that help you feel grounded. Write them down if it helps. For me, time with my family and the practices that keep me calm, like exercise and meditation, are non-negotiables. Knowing what these are makes it easier to recognize when a boundary is being crossed.

2. Start Small

If boundaries are new to you, don't try to change everything at once. Start with manageable steps. Maybe it's saying no to plans when you need rest, or carving out a small window of time each day for yourself.

3. Communicate with Kindness and Firmness

You don't owe anyone a long explanation. A simple, "I need some time to recharge," is enough. People who respect you will understand, and those who don't? That's about them, not you.

4. Let Go with Love

Sometimes, protecting your peace means letting go of relationships or commitments that no longer align with your life. This doesn't have to involve conflict. It can be as simple as stepping back gently, trusting that those who truly care for you will respect your growth.

I'll be honest: setting boundaries isn't always easy. It can feel uncomfortable, and you might face pushback. But every time you honour your needs, you're showing yourself and your family that you're worth protecting.

The life I've built with Sacha and our daughters didn't happen by chance. It came from hard work, from prioritizing what matters, and from learning to say no when needed. And let me tell you, it's worth it.

Your peace is worth it. Your family is worth it. And you are worth it.

MAKING FRIENDS WITH CALM

Growing up, the concept of peace felt alien to me. My early years were marked by frequent moves—before I even turned one, I had lived in five different homes. Stability was a stranger, and chaos my constant companion. It's a familiar story for many who've grown up under similar circumstances. For us, calm can almost feel unsettling, as if it's a void where the chaos used to be.

Even when I started my business in London and began earning more money than ever before, the old patterns of instability lingered. You might think that financial security would bring calm, but instead, I found myself spending money as fast as I earned it, mimicking the financial chaos of my childhood. That whisper from my past always lurking: *Don't get too comfortable—it could all disappear tomorrow.* This wasn't deliberate self-sabotage but an ingrained response to unfamiliar stability.

Realizing this, I began to consciously shift my approach to money—saving, planning, and slowly learning to respect financial stability rather than fear it. But financial habits were just one aspect; this need for chaos seeped into other areas of my life too, like relationships and work, where gossip and mistrust can create unnecessary strife.

The turning point came when I discovered meditation. It was in 2011 at the London Buddhist Centre, where sitting quietly, focusing on my breath, felt initially like an odd disruption of my normal pace. Yet, it became a profound practice for me. Meditation taught me to appreciate calm, not as an empty space, but as a fertile ground for clarity and growth. It taught me that calm is something you embrace, not something you run from.

The benefits of meditation are well-documented. Studies show that regular meditation can significantly reduce stress and improve decision-making abilities by enhancing focus and emotional regulation. For instance, research published in the *Journal of Cognitive Enhancement* suggests that consistent meditation practice leads to improvements in cognitive flexibility and sustained attention, which directly impacts our ability to make thoughtful decisions in everyday life.

If you're struggling to embrace calm, consider weaving moments of meditation into your day. It doesn't have to mean sitting cross-legged in silence (though if that works, great). Meditation can be as simple as creating a few still moments—turning calm from an elusive stranger into a trusted ally.

But let's be honest: if your house is anything like mine, with young children and two dogs, "calm" can feel like a distant dream. Some days, it's like trying to hold onto a greased-up balloon while a circus is in full swing.

That's why I've learned to get creative. For me, walking the dogs in the forest has become a type of meditation. No phone calls, no distractions—just me, the dogs, and Mother Nature (and occasionally a dog rolling in something they shouldn't). It's not perfect, but it works.

Meditation doesn't have to look a certain way. It's about finding your moments of peace, whether it's a quiet minute before the kids wake up, a walk outside, or a few deep breaths in the car. However small, those moments remind you that calm isn't a void—it's a foundation.

So if life feels chaotic, know that you're not alone. Calm is still possible—even in the madness—and when you make space for it, you'll find it gives you clarity, connection, and the strength to keep going.

REFRAMING SELF-SABOTAGE

Self-sabotage isn't always the dramatic, movie-worthy meltdown you might imagine. It doesn't always involve hitting a big red self-destruct button or throwing a hand grenade into the middle of your life. Instead, it's usually something much more subtle—a slow erosion of the daily practices that keep us aligned. It starts when you skip one workout, then another, or when you keep saying, "I'll do it tomorrow," about your journaling or meditating. It's those days you decide to skip therapy or take a break from the routines that keep you happy and grounded.

For me, maintaining a daily routine is crucial for showing up to life as my best self. Every day, I dedicate time to stretch my body for 10 minutes, engage in 10 minutes of breathwork, spend 10 minutes meditating, and wrap up with 5 minutes of gratitude and morning prayers. This routine ensures that I approach life's challenges from the best frame of mind possible. Life is ultimately a series of decisions, and if I show up to each decision in the best frame of mind, I'm more likely to make good choices, leading to a good life. My life, my responsibility.

My self-sabotage wasn't loud or chaotic—it was quiet, almost unnoticeable at first. But over time, those little choices started to add up, pulling me further and further away from the person I wanted to be. I had to find a way to stop that decline, to reframe how I thought about my daily routines.

The turning point came when I asked myself: *Why do I do these things?* Exercise, meditation, breathwork, getting out in nature—I don't do them because *I have* to. I do them because *I choose* to. Why do I choose to do them? Because I want to be happy. That's it. I like feeling happy. And when I'm happy, I'm a better father, a better husband, and life just feels easier.

That simple reframe shifted everything for me. Instead of seeing these habits as obligations, I began to see them as choices that supported the life I wanted to build. And it worked. This method helped me to keep moving forward the best I could, even on the tough days.

It's the same with therapy. I've often had that little voice in my head whispering, *You're fine, Mike. You've been sober for years. Nothing major is going on—why bother?* But I don't go to therapy because I have to. I go because it keeps me on top of my game. I like feeling grounded. I like not living with constant anxiety. And most of all, I like feeling happy.

Reframing my mindset from *have to* to *choose to* has been one of the most effective ways to keep self-sabotage at bay. It reminds me that these routines aren't chores—they're tools to create a life I enjoy living.

So if you find yourself slipping into self-sabotage, ask yourself: *Why do I do these things? Why does it matter to me?* And if the answer is that it makes you happier, calmer, or stronger, let that be your reason. Let that be the thing that keeps you on track.

Now, I know I'm talking a very good game here, but let's be real—I'm far from perfect. I can already hear my wife's voice in the back of my head saying, "*This sounds great, Mike. You should try doing it sometime!*" But this is what it's all about—it's about progress, not perfection. I'm still on this path too. I don't have it all figured out, and I probably never will. But I share these tools with the hope that you find some of them useful on your own journey.

So, ask yourself: Do you like to be happy? If so, what can you do today to contribute towards your own happiness? And remember this: if you choose to do nothing towards your own happiness, then that's your contribution to your unhappiness. Your life, your responsibility—your happiness is your responsibility too.

TIME AND LOVE

In 2015, after attending an enlightening event about father-son relationships, I was inspired to reach out to my father, despite knowing the challenges we both faced. He was deep in the throes of heroin addiction, living in a shared house with other addicts—a setting fraught with instability. Despite this, I felt a pull to reconnect, to try and salvage whatever bond we could.

The initial attempt to contact him was itself a journey through the realities of addiction. I texted an old number, hoping it would still connect me to him. The response I received, "Who is this?" and the follow-up, "I don't have a son called Michael," was a harsh reminder of the chaos that addiction can bring into lives. It turned out the phone had been sold to fund drug habits—a common scenario in the world of addiction. Thankfully, the person who answered passed along another number, which finally reached my father.

Sending that message felt like casting a line across a vast ocean of past hurts and disappointments: "Hi Dad, it's Michael, your son. Just wanting to check in, see how you are, and hopefully reconnect." The wait for a reply was agonizing, filled with every possible emotion from hope to fear. Then, his response came through, simple yet profound, "I love you son, I'm sorry I haven't been there, let's meet up for a cup of tea." My heart surged with a mixture of joy and a daunting realization of the long road ahead.

Setting boundaries was crucial from the outset. When we met, I laid them out clearly: no contact while under the influence, no financial support to feed his addiction, and no need for lies—I loved him regardless of his recovery status. These boundaries were not just for my protection but for the integrity and viability of any relationship we might salvage.

Our interactions, framed by these boundaries, allowed us to build a form of relationship that had been impossible in the years lost to his addiction. He sometimes tested these limits, asking for money, and each time I had to remind him why I could not comply. Yet, I supported him in other ways, ensuring he had food and essentials. This wasn't just about setting rules; it was about building a safe space for both of us.

The next four years were a mix of simple joys and ongoing challenges. We shared meals, conversations, and moments of quiet understanding. His message during my book tour, telling me he was proud of me, was a high point, marking how far we had come. His passing in July 2019, just two weeks after the publication of my life story, was bittersweet. It brought our journey to a close—a journey marked by tentative reconnection and cautious hope.

At his funeral, surrounded by siblings I had never known, I was inundated with questions about the man he was. Despite the pain and the complexity of his life, I realized the boundaries we had set gave us both a precious gift: time. Time that many of my siblings did not get to share with him. For those four years, we had something resembling peace, a relationship that allowed us to express love within the safety of clear limits.

Reflecting on the journey I shared with my father in his final years, I've come to understand a profound, lasting peace that lingers in the heart long after someone has passed. This peace comes from knowing you did all you could within the boundaries that protected both your well-being and that of the relationship.

When we consider peace, it's often about the calm we strive for in our current lives, but there's also a deep, enduring peace that comes after someone is gone. It stems from having built bridges, not walls, with thoughtful boundaries that kept us safe. In my own experience, setting clear boundaries with my father—like ensuring we didn't interact when he was under the influence and not providing financial support that could contribute to his addiction—allowed us to reconnect in a meaningful yet safe way. These weren't just barriers; they were the very framework that supported the last years of a relationship that could have otherwise felt unresolved.

If there's someone you've distanced yourself from, consider what boundaries would need to be in place to safely renew that connection. What would those boundaries look like? How would they help protect you and your loved ones while opening a door to potential reconciliation?

Reconnecting doesn't mean forgetting the reasons why you distanced yourself in the first place; it's about managing the relationship in a way that maintains your integrity and safety. It's worth pondering if there's a way to extend a bridge, albeit with guardrails firmly in place, to ensure everyone involved is respected and protected.

This reflection isn't just about seeking peace with others—it's also about finding peace within yourself. So, take a moment to think about the relationships in your life. If there's a bridge to be rebuilt, how can you do it wisely, ensuring it's strong enough to support both reconciliation and your well-being?

THE LEGACY OF PEACE

When you live in peace, it's not just for you—it ripples out to everyone around you. Your children, your loved ones, your community—they all feel the impact of your calm presence. You become an example of what's possible, a living reminder that peace isn't some far-off dream. It's a choice we make every day, moment by moment.

Legacy isn't about the material things we leave behind. It's about how we live, the example we set, and the foundation we build for those who come after us. For me, this hits close to home. Both my parents were alcoholics and addicts, and the chaos that came with that shaped so much of my early life. When I became a parent, I made a promise to myself: the cycle ends here.

My daughters have never seen me drink or use drugs. They've never had to tiptoe around an unpredictable home, waiting for the next outburst or argument. They've never had to question whether they're safe, loved, or wanted. That's what breaking cycles looks like—it's creating a new normal, a home where peace, love, and stability are the foundation.

But let me be clear: it's not about being perfect. I don't always get it right, and I know I never will. Breaking cycles isn't about becoming flawless—it's about showing up, being present, and doing the best you can to create an environment where peace can thrive. It's about making different choices, even when it's hard, because you know the generations that follow will build on what you create today.

Imagine if each of us, as parents, aimed to make our homes just a little more stable, loving, and peaceful than the ones we grew up in. Somewhere along the line in our human history, we forgot a fundamental duty—to protect the weak and vulnerable and to respect Mother Earth. I'm calling us to remember and act on this basic principle. Think about a world where every generation carries forward less pain and more hope. It's about creating a safe and nurturing space not just for our children but for all who are vulnerable—the women, the children, the elderly, and not forgetting our planet itself. This isn't about leaving behind wealth or possessions, but about breaking the cycles of chaos and choosing calm, choosing love. When I think about this, I think of my daughters. My goal isn't to make their lives perfect—it's to show them what's possible. To give them a home where they feel safe, loved, and encouraged to be themselves. A home where they can grow into the kind of people who will carry that sense of peace into the world.

And it's not just about family. The way we show up in our communities, the way we treat strangers, the way we respond to conflict—it all matters. Living in peace is one of the greatest gifts we can give, not just to ourselves but to everyone we meet.

If enough of us commit to this—to choosing peace, protecting it, and nurturing it—we might just create a world where peace isn't the exception but the rule.

IT'S NOT ABOUT US—IT'S ABOUT OTHERS

At some point in this journey, we come to realise something profound: it's not just about us. All the pain we've endured, all the lessons we've learned, all the work we've done—it's not meant to stay with us. It's meant to be shared, recycled, and used to help others.

When we take the pain we've carried and turn it into something that can uplift, inspire, or heal someone else, we transform not only our own lives but the lives of those around us. That's how we grow as individuals, and that's how we evolve as a species—one generation at a time, passing forward a little less pain and a little more hope.

This isn't about being perfect or trying to save the world. It's about showing up in the lives of others with authenticity and vulnerability. It's about sharing your story, your lessons, your truth, and trusting that someone, somewhere, will hear it and feel less alone.

For me, recycling my pain has become a way of life. Whether it's stepping into a circle to lead or stepping into the middle of one to do my own work, I've come to understand that everything I've endured has value—not just for me, but for others. Every moment of darkness, every hard-earned victory, every mistake, and every breakthrough becomes a tool for connection, a way to bridge the gap between human hearts.

And this isn't just about the people closest to us. It's about the strangers we meet, the communities we serve, and the generations that follow. Imagine what the world could look like if each of us committed to breaking even one cycle of pain in our own lives. Imagine the ripple effect if every parent created a home that was just a little more loving, more stable, and more peaceful than the one they grew up in.

This is how we evolve—by taking the lessons from our pain and turning them into something beautiful, something useful, something that can guide someone else on their own journey. It's not about us. It's about others.

So, ask yourself: What can I do with my experience? How can I use what I've learned to help someone else? Because when we choose to share, to serve, and to show up for others, we become part of something bigger than ourselves. I want to emphasize this: even if the only change you make is creating a better life for your children, that alone is one of the greatest acts of service you can offer—to yourself, your family, and humanity as a whole. Imagine if every parent committed to this. Within just one generation, we would see a vastly transformed and improved human experience.

This is how we grow. This is how we heal. This is how we change the world—one story, one lesson, one generation at a time.

AN INVITATION TO CHANGE

As we come to the end of this book, I want to take a moment to say goodbye—not just to close the pages but to truly honour the journey we've walked together. This hasn't just been a collection of words. It's been a shared experience, a deep dive into the hard truths, the quiet reflections, and the hope for something better. It hasn't been an easy road, but you've stayed with it. You've dared to look inward, to sit with your pain, and to believe—even in the smallest ways—that change is possible.

This book wasn't written by someone who had all the answers. I didn't grow up in a safe, stable home. My life was chaos—some of it inherited, some of it self-inflicted. If you'd told me years ago that I'd be here, writing to you about healing, peace, and transformation, I would have laughed in your face.

Yet, here I am.

And that's the point, isn't it? If this kind of life is possible for me, it's possible for you too.

When I started writing this book, I wanted to share the path that brought me here. Together, we've walked through the foundations of my journey towards a better life. We started with safety because no real growth can happen without it. We faced our hidden truths, shining a light on the parts of ourselves we'd tried to bury. We confronted pain, not to erase it but to release it. We found connection, reminding ourselves that healing doesn't happen in isolation but in relationship with others. We focused on integration, taking what we've learned and applying it to our daily lives. And finally, we arrived at peace—not as a destination, but as a choice we make every single day.

This journey isn't about becoming perfect. It's about integrating all the parts of ourself we may have suppressed or denied. It's about learning to live in a way that honours your truth, your needs, and your values. It's about embracing all of who we are—the light and the dark, the tri- umphs and the stumbles—and knowing that every piece of us belongs.

For me, this journey has led to a life I never dreamed possible. I live in Devon on the Blackdown Hills, with my wife, Sacha, and our daughters. We have dogs, chickens, and seven beehives. Our summers are spent walking along the stream at the bottom of our field, the sound of the water mixing with the laughter of our girls. My wife and children have never seen me drunk.

This is what change looks like.

It's a far cry from the council estate in Isleworth where I grew up—surrounded by chaos, believing that peace was something other people had but not me. I don't share this to make myself sound great. I share it because I know how rare this life is. I know the reality of the community I came from, where many never get the chance to live a life like this.

That's why I wrote this book. I want us all to win. I want to raise the bottom, to change the systems that failed me and so many others. I dream of a world where healing isn't a privilege but a right.

The journey through the seven stages of healing from trauma isn't easy, but every step brings you closer to the freedom you deserve. These are the steps I took to heal my trauma, and I hope you've found something within these pages to help you with yours.

When doubt creeps in, remember this: the fact that you're here, daring to believe in change, is proof of your strength.

So this is my final farewell. Writing this book feels like closing a chapter—not just in my story, but in the work I began with *Young Offender*. That book was about where I came from; this one is about what's possible. Together, they tell a story of transformation. And with this book, that story feels complete.

If you'd like to connect with me beyond this book, you can. You'll find me out here, continuing this work, believing wholeheartedly in the power of change. Truth is, you won't find me constantly posting on social media, promoting myself or what I do. I'm too busy out here actually doing it—living the life I speak about in this book.

So, if you notice I'm quiet online, know that's the reason why. I'm not sitting on the sidelines; I'm in the trenches, working with people, helping those who feel unseen and unheard, and dedicating my time to the mission that means everything to me.

If you want to connect, come and join one of the events with the organisations I'm affiliated with. That's where the real work happens—in person, face-to-face, in spaces where healing, growth, and transformation are possible.

And if our paths never cross, I want you to know this: I've dedicated my life to this mission. Until my final breath, I'll be here—fighting for change, offering hope where it's needed most, and standing alongside those whose voices are so often unheard.

Let this give you hope. Hope that someone is out there, in the trenches, fighting for those whose stories rarely make headlines, for those in poor schools and forgotten communities across the UK. And know this—I'm not alone. There are many of us doing this work, quietly and tirelessly, even if you don't hear about us.

Let this remind you that change is coming. The fact that you're reading this book is proof of that. The great awakening is already taking place. Together, we are part of something bigger, something capable of creating real and lasting change.

That change is fuelled by something powerful, something deep within us all—the human spirit. It's a force no one can take away from us, no matter how broken the systems, how poorly our governments are run, or how heavy the burdens of wars, pandemics, and terrorism may feel. There is something stronger than all of that, : the human spirit.

It's the spirit that kept me going all these years, through all the darkness, to bring this book to you. It's unyielding and unbreakable, and it's what reminds us that, no matter how overwhelming life gets, the light is always within us— and we have the power to share it with the world.

We didn't come this far to play small. We are here to create something meaningful, to turn our pain into purpose, and to live a life that inspires—not just us, but those around us too.

Because when we heal ourselves, we create ripples that touch the lives of others. One person, one family, one community at a time, we help to heal the world.

So keep going and keep believing.

With all my love and gratitude,

Michael

ACKNOWLEDGEMENTS

To my wife, Sacha—thank you for your patience, love, and understanding as I've walked this path of healing. You've stood beside me through the chaos and the calm, holding space for me when I couldn't hold it for myself. Your love has been my anchor, and your belief in me has kept me grounded. You've taught me more about resilience and grace than I ever thought possible. I couldn't have done any of this without you.

To my daughters—Connie, Sienna, and Savanna— thank you for being my greatest teachers. Watching you grow has been the most profound and humbling experience of my life. You have shown me the true meaning of love, patience, and purpose.

To Sean C—my first sponsor and mentor. You helped me get sober in 2007, and in doing so, you saved my life. Your honesty, guidance, and unwavering support gave me a foundation to build on when I didn't know where to start. I carry your wisdom with me every day, and I hope this book honours the gift you gave me.

To my dad, Kevin—thank you for the lessons in for-giveness and compassion. Our time together was brief, but in those years leading up to your death, I learned what it means to let go of resentment and lean into connection.

Those memories will stay with me always, and I'm grateful for them.

To my mum— Thank you for finding the courage to get sober—it was your strength that led me to my own sobriety. This book wouldn't exist if you hadn't made that life-changing decision. The beautiful memories we've created since then mean everything to me. Your love, resilience, and example have shaped my journey, and for that, I am forever grateful.

Donnie Dhillon - my business coach, for always supporting my endeavours and everything I do. Your guidance, belief in me, and constant encouragement have been instrumental in helping me build not just a business, but a life I'm proud of. Thank you for always having my back and pushing me to reach heights I once thought were impossible.

To Duane and Catherine O'Kane—your work and support helped Sacha and me navigate the depths of my trauma and find a way to rebuild. The tools you gave us have transformed not just my life but the lives of so many others. Your impact will always be part of my journey.

To The Mankind Project—for creating a space where I could question everything I thought I knew about being a man. You gave me the courage to redefine masculinity and find my way back to my truth. That space changed me, and I'll forever be grateful for it.

To Antony Eldridge Rogers—your mentorship since I moved to Devon has been a guiding light. The wisdom you've shared about fatherhood, marriage, and life has shaped how I show up for my family and myself. Your kindness, patience, and insight have left a lasting impact on my life.

To Dame Carol Black-Thank you for believing in me, the work I do, and this book. Your unwavering dedication to bringing about change within our government has been truly inspiring. The impact of your work is felt far and wide, and it's been an honour to walk alongside someone as committed to making a difference as you are.

To Thomas Hal Robson-Kanu-Thank you for believing in me, this message, and this book. Thank you for looking beyond the label of a convicted armed robber and seeing the man I have worked hard to become—the man who is striving to do good in the world. Your belief in me has meant more than words can say, and I am deeply grateful for your support.

To Chris Wallwork—thank you for the hours spent sitting across from me in therapy, guiding me through the darkest corners of my past. Your compassion and skill helped me process pain I didn't know how to face, and because of you, I've started to believe I deserve the life I'm building.

To my incredible team at The CIP Project—you are the heart of everything we do. Without your passion and dedication, none of this would be possible. Thank you for believing in the work and helping us make real change in the world.

To Andy Walker and Justin Maisey—thank you for stepping into Oakhill and carrying it forward so I could pursue this work. Your support has given my family stability, and your generosity in filtering some of the business's success into The CIP Project speaks volumes about the kind of men you are.

To all the team at Oakhill Estate Agents—Jusdeep, James, Harsh, Kalina, Emily, and Nina—thank you for all your hard work, dedication, and the energy you bring every day. Your efforts don't go unnoticed, and I'm deeply grateful for each of you.

To Simon Cavaciuti – Thank you for your friendship, your unwavering encouragement, and your steadfast belief in this book. Your support has meant more to me than I can ever express. You've been a sounding board, a motivator, and a reminder that this story needed to be told.

To Anne Main – Thank you for helping my mum get sober, which in turn helped me find my own path to sobriety. Your kindness, loyalty, and unwavering support of our family and my work with CIP over the years have meant more than words can express. I am eternally grateful for everything you've done and the role you've played in our journey.

To the Lakota, Blackfoot, and Shoshone-Bannock peoples of America. Your teachings on life, spirituality, and the essence of living well have been invaluable in shaping my path. Thank you for your profound impact on my journey and for guiding me with your wisdom and spirit.

And to God—thank you for never giving up on me, even when I gave up on myself. For the times I turned to you in desperation and for the times I've come to you with gratitude since I got sober in 2007. You've been my guide, my source of strength, and my reminder that even in the darkest moments, there's always hope.

POEMS BY MICHAEL MAISEY

MY LONELY PRISON WALL

The echoes linger, trapped in the stone,
Voices of boys who felt so alone.
In this cell where shadows fall,
I hear the whispers through the wall.

Young men who slept, their final breath,
Detoxing bodies surrendering to death.
This was their tomb, a bed too small,
Now marked forever on this prison wall.

This was my cell, my living grave,
A place where no one could hear or save.
At eighteen years, my soul so frail,
I rolled up the bed sheets to bid farewell.

The bars loomed high, the rope was tight,
And the whispers crept in, cloaked in spite.
"You're a waste of space," they hissed with glee,
"Do us all a favour; set yourself free."

The bed sheets held, the noose pulled tight,
And my body gave way to the endless night.
I felt my breath slip, my mind grow still,
And whispered my goodbyes against my will.

"Sorry, Mum, I couldn't be more,
Sorry, Justin, for closing this door.
If I had one chance, just one more day,
I'd change it all—but it's too late to stay."

But then, through the dark, a flicker, a spark,
A light broke through the endless dark.
The bars seemed to shake, the whispers to cease,
And in the stillness, I heard, "Choose peace."

I woke from the abyss, gasping for air,
Still alive in my cell, stripped but aware.
That lonely wall, a witness to pain,
Became the ground where I'd rise again.

Feltham's stone holds the cries of the lost,
Boys like me who paid the cost.
But in that cell, I found my fight,
A spark of hope in the darkest night.

Now, I see that wall, not as my end,
But as a place where I began to mend.
To every boy who feels so small,
I stand here free, beyond that wall.

You're not a waste, you're not alone,
Your story's not over—it's still your own.
The whispers may haunt, the darkness may call,
But there's a life waiting beyond the wall.

Michael Maisey

THE GIFT OF THE WORK

In quiet corners of the world so wide,
Whispers of truth where secrets hide.
Not in grand stages, under spotlight's glow,
But in soft shadows, where few dare to go.

There once lived a man, burdened and worn,
Whose heart had been tattered, weathered, and torn.
He stumbled upon a path, barely seen,
Where the work of healing washed his spirit clean.

This wasn't a task of simple repair,
But a journey to face what was hidden there.
With each small step, and each tear that fell,
He learned of his stories that pain did tell.

The work, it asked for courage, deep and true,
To embrace the grief and let it pass through.
In silence, he found a strength untold,
His heart rebuilt, strong and bold

It was in connection, reaching out to another,
Finding solace in the soul of a brother.
In the quietest moments, under soft starlight,
He discovered the power to fight the good fight.

Now, this wasn't easy; the path was steep,
Lined with memories that made him weep.
But with each weeping wound that he did mend,
A little more light through the cracks would bend.

So here's to the work, a journey so profound,
Where true freedom and love are found.
For every tear shed, every burden borne,
Is a step toward the light, the break of dawn.

Yet as he healed, a truth became clear,
This sacred work, to his heart so dear,
Should never be sold, never be priced,
For its value in gold could never suffice.

This gift from above, from the divine,
Was not just his to hold or define.
It saved his life, gave him new breath,
A beacon of hope in a world shadowed by death.

Let us not turn this journey, so heartfelt and true,
Into a commodity, something to sell or accrue.
For this healing is priceless, it's pure and it's right,
To spread freely as day follows night.

Here, we pledge this work, this sacred call,
To be accessible to one and all.
Rich or poor, in wealth or in strife,
Everyone deserves the chance for a better life.

So, if you're wandering, lost in the night,
Look for the path with the softest light.
It's there you'll find what you need to thrive,
The work to help your soul come alive.

Michael Maisey

FOR MY DAUGHTERS

I look at you, my precious girls,
stepping out into this big world.
A realm of wonder, beauty, and strife,
I hope I've prepared you for this life.

Your sacred strength, your gentle might,
have taught me more about what's right.
Please trust the voice within,
and stand firm when storms begin.

My heart holds fears, soft and deep,
my sadness stirs as I watch you leap.
Towards futures where I cannot go,
knowing one day you'll leave our home.

I've laboured hard to break old chains,
in our home, only love remains.
Where you are cherished, valued, heard,
and shining brightly is not deterred.

Yet the world is vast, and I but one,
I pray for the partners you might one day love.
May they be gentle, kind, and true,
men who are loyal to only you.

Men who've healed, who've faced their fears,
who stand unafraid of your strength, my dears.
For a good man honors the sacred divine,
and sees in your eyes his guiding light.

I pray for laughter that knows no tears,
for a life where your beauty only grows each year.
But if shadows fall and try to dim your way,
remember your fire, as bright as day.

You are whole and strong, your spirits brave,
just like the gentle sound of waves.
These lessons you've taught, with gentle hands,
remind me where real strength stands.

Your light remains a beacon true,
through all life's trials, it carries you.
Though I may not see all you become,
in your kindness, my heart is won.

For you are my hope, my love, my prayer,
your journeys far, yet I am there.
My legacy lies not just in your grace and drive,
but in the love and purpose you bring to life.

Michael Maisey

RESOURCES

Embarking on a journey of personal growth and transformation is greatly enriched by access to supportive resources and communities. This section outlines how you can work with me and highlights organizations I'm affiliated with. Additionally, it includes recommendations for other valuable groups that provide training and support based on my personal and professional experiences.

WORKING WITH ME AND MY AFFILIATED ORGANIZATIONS

CROI CONNECTIONS, IRELAND

Set up by Helen and Alan O'Brien, Croi Connections is an organization dedicated to fostering deep personal connections and growth through workshops and community engagement, with a focus on holistic individual development. Both Helen and Alan trained with The CIP Project in the methods we use, and Alan is also a qualified therapist. They are lovely, family-oriented people who deeply care about their community. We hold events close to Newgrange, the sacred burial site in Ireland, to honour our Irish ancestors and sacred traditions, integrating these profound cultural elements into our programs. Website: www.croiconnections.ie

MANTRA MENSWORK, SCOTLAND

Founded by David Ross Millar, a good friend, devoted husband, and father, Mantra Menswork focuses on men's development. The organization offers transformative workshops and support groups that encourage men to explore and express their emotions and vulnerabilities within a nurturing environment. Mantra Menswork combines expert-led programs that foster personal growth and community among men. As part of the leadership team, I actively facilitate at all of their full weekend events, helping to guide and support participants through their transformative journeys.

Website: www.mantramenswork.com

THE CIP PROJECT, ENGLAND

Founded by myself, The CIP Project is a charity that operates across the UK, providing vital support and resources to nearly 2000 individuals annually in prisons and schools. Our focus is on healing, personal growth, and preventing re-offending through innovative workshops and training. We offer our services not only within the prison system but also through free online support and at our 25-acre outdoor retreat centre in Devon. This makes our work accessible to anyone who needs it, employing all the methods discussed in this book to facilitate transformation and support.

Website: www.thecipproject.com

SUGGESTED ORGANIZATIONS FOR TRAINING AND SUPPORT

CLEARMIND INTERNATIONAL

Founded by Duane and Catherine O'Kane, Clearmind International offers transformative educational experiences, workshops, and training programs that help individuals explore emotional health and relational well-being. Both Duane and Catherine are qualified therapists who pioneered the relational work that forms the core of Clearmind's programs. This work has had a profound impact on many, including myself and my wife, Sacha. Sacha completed a one-year training course in counselling with them, which speaks to the powerful and effective nature of their approach.

Website: www.clearmind.com

THE MANKIND PROJECT UK AND IRELAND

The Mankind Project UK and Ireland is truly at the heart of men's development, dedicated to fostering emotional maturity and personal integrity through their training programs, mentorship, and community service initiatives. They help men to live authentically and connect deeply with others. To me, MKP stands as the original pioneers of men's work. They have profoundly influenced my journey, providing invaluable insights and tools that helped me redefine what masculinity means. Their approach has shown me how to embrace vulnerability and strength simultaneously, reshaping my understanding and expression of what it is to be a man

Website: www.mankindproject.org.uk

WIM HOF BREATHWORK

Developed by Wim Hof, this method of breathwork is now recognized globally for its powerful and transformative effects. The Wim Hof Method combines controlled exposure to cold and specific breathing exercises that have been scientifically proven to improve physical and mental health. This approach not only boosts immunity but also enhances emotional resilience, helping practitioners gain a greater control over their body's responses to stress and environmental challenges.

Website: www.wimhofmethod.com

THE LONDON BUDDHIST CENTRE

The London Buddhist Centre offers courses, retreats, and workshops in meditation, mindfulness, and Buddhism, providing tools for living a happier, more peaceful life and fostering a supportive community. This centre has been instrumental in my journey, helping me to deeply understand meditation and the power of the mind. The teachings I've absorbed there have enabled me to live more peacefully, giving me practical strategies to manage stress and enhance my daily life through mindfulness and spiritual growth.

Website: www.lbc.org.uk

THE SOVEREIGN'S JOURNEY

Founded by Hugh Newton, whom I have looked up to as an elder for many years, The Sovereign's Journey offers programs focused on personal sovereignty and leadership.

Hugh has been instrumental in training the staff at my organization, The CIP Project, helping individuals navigate their paths with clarity and purpose.

Website: www.thesovereignsjourney.co.uk

HTS ORGANISATION

Led by Rod Boothroyd and Marianne Hill, both pioneers in the field of shadow work in the UK, HTS Organisation offers training and development programs that enhance individuals' skills and capabilities across various aspects of personal and professional life. For those interested in deepening their understanding of shadow work, I highly recommend checking out Rod Boothroyd's books, which provide valuable insights into this transformative approach.

Website: www.htsorganisation.co.uk

Each of these organizations provides unique resources and communities that can support you on your path. Whether you are looking for direct coaching, group workshops, or self-led practices, these organizations offer a wealth of knowledge and support to guide you. Engaging with these resources can be a profound step toward personal transformation and a more fulfilled life.

Printed in Dunstable, United Kingdom